Finance in Your Church

Finance
in
Your
Church

Douglas W. Johnson

Abingdon Press
Nashville

Finance in Your Church

Copyright © 1986 by Abingdon Press

This book is printed on acid-free paper.

Library of Congress Cataloging-in-Publication Data

JOHNSON, DOUGLAS W.
    Finance in your church.   1. Church finance. 2. Stewardship, Christian.
    I. Title
    BT770.J64   1986   254.8   86-10709

ISBN 0-687-12987-7 (soft: alk. paper)

MANUFACTURED BY THE PARTHENON PRESS AT
NASHVILLE, TENNESSEE, UNITED STATES OF AMERICA

PREFACE

How many times I have wanted a book to use or to hand to a pastor to answer a question about finances in the church! An Abingdon Press editor felt that this need was more than mine alone. This book, written at his suggestion, is my effort to bring existing knowledge about finances in the church into a single volume.

The book is based on the learning of people whose lives have been spent raising money and teaching stewardship. Their insights have been filed away without footnotes because they have talked to me and guided me during my research. To these persons I owe very much, and I extend to them my personal thanks.

It is hoped that what follows will answer many pastors' questions about church finances and guide them toward better stewardship in the church and in their personal lives.

DOUGLAS W. JOHNSON
Ridgewood, New Jersey
December 1985

CONTENTS

INTRODUCTION

Pastors are beset with problems and confronted by opportunities when it comes to finances in the church. People need theological advice about making money as well as guidelines for using and giving it. Church leaders who raise money through gimmicks, raffles, and lotteries in secular situations, need to learn the difference between secular and church money-raising techniques and rationales. Church members, in church and secular situations, need to be taught the concepts of stewardship.

The responses of pastors to problems of fundraising, as well as their opportunities to define the differences between secular and Christian uses of money, often depend on how quickly they can secure information. Pastors need information in order to suggest alternative ways to meet problems. They need guidance and resources in order to help people who want to give to the church.

Frequently, pastors do not have time to make exhaustive or even cursory searches for available information. They do not know of the resources that they can use or suggest to lay persons. In addition to lack of time, most pastors do not have budgets large enough to purchase many books and materials, or to collect other forms of information related to various aspects of personal and church finance.

This book endeavors to satisfy a pastor's basic needs. It brings together the kinds of information a pastor needs on the spur of the moment to answer questions or to make suggestions to church leaders or members. It seeks to help pastors meet immediate needs and act on current opportunities regarding finances in the church. It describes aspects of various issues relating to church finances. These descriptions include evaluation of approaches to fund raising.

This book is also designed for easy reference. It is divided into four parts, each of which brings together related topics. Each topic is discussed separately by chapter and each is based upon the types of questions people ask pastors about church finances.

A list of resources, including the addresses of certain denominational offices, follows the closing chapter. Staff members of these offices can be quite helpful in pointing to resources or responding to urgent questions. Furthermore, they can usually be accessed quickly, and generally have relevant information to share over the telephone.

Finance
in
Your
Church

Chapter 1

FINANCE AND THEOLOGY

"The way people make and spend money reflects their personality."

"What do you mean by that?"

"Well. . . I mean that people's life-styles can be described by looking at their checkbooks. The way they spend their money tells volumes about them. For instance, a person who spends a lot on hotel fares, taxi cabs, and airplane tickets will have a different outlook on life than someone who stays within ten miles of his or her birthplace for a lifetime. As another example, a person who spends more on entertainment than on education or food may be considered, by an individual whose money is spent primarily on personal development, to be addicted to escapism, hedonism, or play acting."

"I've heard life-styles described this way before but haven't given it much thought. Let's see . . . as I think back over our family's spending this past month, someone could tell quite a bit about our life patterns. For example, we were willing to pay taxes to live in this community, we supported a church, we paid some education bills, and we made some charges during a two-day vacation. I guess if you were to look at an entire year our spending could tell you a lot about our life-style. In fact, I'd venture to suggest that there is a strong relationship between spending and theology."

"You certainly took a big jump from where I started. I was talking about life-style and you take up theology!"

"Theology is a part of one's life-style, isn't it?"

"I haven't thought about it in those terms. You are saying that my beliefs about God, or lack of beliefs, affect how I live. That does seem reasonable."

"Theology might be a jump ahead of where you began, but a person's beliefs greatly affect how money is used. As I see it, the relationship between money and life-style is a theological issue."

These two pastors are struggling with the relationship between money and theology. This relationship is not generally discussed in seminary, but it becomes an issue when pastors are confronted by the need to help raise money to finance the operations of a church. Pastors are trained in theology, Bible, and the church's need to interact with its environment, before they get into the parish. As they become pastor of a church, they discover they have neither the experience nor the background to deal theologically with finance. Consequently, as they begin their career, pastors must develop an ethical and theological framework for church finance in order to function well in this arena.

Creating such a framework should not be a dilemma for most pastors. When they are forced to consider, in the crucible of trying to raise money for the church, the theology of church finance, they will discover they must create a personal life-style that connects theology with money. This need to work out a theology of personal finance will benefit pastors personally as well as contribute positively toward creating a theology of church finance.

Connecting theology with money can be difficult however for those pastors who readily accept the profit motive, but who de-emphasize ethical considerations about the ways one acquires and uses money. Establishing a connection between theology and money is also difficult for pastors who consider money an evil force or a necessary evil. Both of these types of pastors tend to ignore their need to think about money in theological terms. Either of these attitudes makes it hard for pastors to develop a realistic theology of finance.

A pastor harboring one of these attitudes will find it difficult to minister to his or her congregation. Church members rely on their pastor to help them think about money theologically. They need theological guidance from the pastor as they acquire and use money. Lay persons have been taught to think of money in nontheological terms. This secularized background makes it difficult for pastors to discuss with them theological concepts about money, such as stewardship.

A pastor must therefore develop an ethic of money acquisition and use before he or she can converse intelligently about money with people who think of money only in secular terms. If a pastor cannot convey a theology of finance, lay persons will not be challenged or confronted with the need to use money for God's purposes.

A theology of finance is important because it accomplishes three tasks: (1) it provides a theological basis of decision making for people who are deciding whether to contribute to the church; (2) it guides financial officers of the church as they design appeals and uses for money in behalf of the congregation; and (3) it acts as a platform of instruction a pastor may use to educate lay persons about a Christian's acquisition and use of money.

People trained in stewardship who think about giving to the church are always confronted with one or more of three issues: the amount of money they can afford to give, the amount of time in addition to money they can contribute, and the amount of accumulated assets that they can offer either as endowments or as memorials for someone in the family. These points are crucial to every potential contributor to the church, regardless of age or financial situation.

Once contributions are received, a theology of finance should guide financial officers in the use of them. This theology must be developed, shared, and established through meetings and from the pulpit by the pastor. The pastor, who has been trained to think theologically, is the primary source of information and training for church leaders as they seek to develop their own theological basis for handling resources.

A theology of finance, properly conceived and presented, should help church members understand how giving money and money equivalents, such as time or property, is integral to their belief systems; it should help trustees, treasurers, and stewardship-finance committees build budgets and create spending patterns; and, it should aid in the solicitation and offering of memorial gifts, wills, and other kinds of contributions.

THEOLOGY AND THE GIVER

Deciding how much to give to the church is important not only to the individual giver but to the church as well. The church depends on regular gifts from members to support its programs and to promote its outreach ministries. Individuals want to do their share to support the church and its outreach ministries. This combination of church need and individual commitment has given rise to much discussion of ways to decide how much to give to the church.

Most literature on this subject suggests proportionate giving. This means an individual reviews his or her personal budget and, based on feelings of commitment to God through the church, decides what percentage of income should be given to the church. This decision should be made when the church shares its proposed annual budget. In secular terms, the process of defining what proportion of one's income is to be given to the church is known as deciding the percent of income that goes to charitable causes—the church, in this case, the charitable cause.

FINANCE AND THEOLOGY

Historically emphasized and based on proportionate giving has been the tithe, defined as one-tenth of one's income. There has been confusion among some advocates of the tithe as to whether the one-tenth should be based on gross or net income. Most advocates, however, justify this form of deciding how to contribute because it is used in the Bible. The tithe, regardless of whether it is based on net or gross income, is easy to compute and saves people the task of finding another formula. For many church people, the fact that the tithe is mentioned in the Bible makes it theologically sound.

A third way to decide how much to contribute is to give whatever one feels like putting into the collection tray when it comes by each week. This method is usually based on emotion since it involves one's overall feelings about the service at the time. Most pastors discourage this method of deciding since it has few theological arguments to support it.

Theologically, giving to the church expresses a person's commitment to God through Christ. Gifts, regardless of whether they are money or time, are personal expressions of commitment to the church. It is important to understand that giving time and talent is as important as contributing money. In effect, giving time means contributors are redirecting their talents to accomplish something for the church in the name of Christ.

Giving, for most Christians, is done primarily in the church. This is expected by church leaders and pastors. Indeed, materials stressing this expectation are produced regularly by denomination offices and distributed by a church during each year's fund-raising campaign. It is theologically acceptable, however, for Christians to give to people or groups that are not a part of the church. Donating to such groups, because of what these groups do, may be a valid alternative expression of an individual's commitment to Christ. Evaluating the nature of other organizations and their purposes however makes giving to nonchurch groups and individuals difficult for church people. It is simpler to follow the inclination to give to the church because they believe in what it does and they feel that the money will be used well.

Wanting to express one's commitment to God is grounded in an individual's personal theology. People's belief systems are their operative theology even though they may not acknowledge having any theology of giving. Many church people have created their operative theology by the time they reach their teenage years. It is largely this age group that a pastor must reach if he or she is to influence their lifetime theology through personal example and preaching.

The pastor has a primary responsibility to help people work through their operating theology in order to create a theology of giving. This means a pastor must emphasize the need for them to express their commitment to Christ through giving to the church. Since this is the primary way many people engage in ministry and service, they should be challenged to contribute money and time to support the church's ministries. The pastor may base his or her teaching on proportionate giving or the tithe.

THEOLOGY AND CHURCH FINANCES

Many pastors want lay persons whose vocations are in finance to chair the church's finance committee. The pastor's implicit, if not explicit, hope is that these people will bring a "businesslike" atmosphere to church finances. These pastors assume that handling business finances is the same as working with church finances.

A theology of church finance makes no such assumption. In the best sense, church finances require an understanding of and commitment to stewardship. After all, church members give their money to build up the church and help people around the world. Donations, to most church members, are for contributing food to the hungry, giving clothes to the ragged, and offering shelter to the homeless.

Church financial officers whose vocations are in finance often believe they must make a profit or hold money in reserve for future bad years. A sound theology of finance opposes this viewpoint. Theologically speaking, the church is a conduit, not a holding company, for contributions. Funds received, therefore, must be carefully recorded and then carefully spent. When a contributor puts money into a collection plate, that person expects results, not dividends or savings fund balances.

A sound theology of church finance requires a balance between conservatism and risk. Risk occurs when the finance committee authorizes spending. Conservatism, as practiced by church leaders, requires that enough money be kept in the accounts to support the church in slow times of vacations and low attendance. The balance between risk and conservatism will result, at the end of a year, in a near zero account level in the benevolence and general funds. Not many business managers feel comfortable with this type of finance.

THEOLOGY FOR HANDLING BEQUESTS

Accumulated resources, money coming from wills and bequests, are different from the money given for current expenses each week or month by living church members. The aim of a bequest is that a specific task or activity be undertaken by the church. In many situations these tasks or activities tend to aggrandize the giver rather than further the purpose of the church. In other cases, the bequest is to be used to minister in a neighborhood desperately needing the church's witness.

Church financial officers have the power to accept or reject a bequest. Relatively few churches are willing to reject money given in this fashion, even though the bequest may, for example, specify that it is to be used to build an unneeded chapel or install another organ. When bequests are involved, theology becomes less important than the amount being offered or the family of the donor.

A theology of finance however insists that each bequest meet the purpose of the church and extend one of its primary goals. Such a theology puts each kind of gift from members into a context of commitment and ministry. As a result, money must be given to enhance the church's various ministries, and when it is not the church's finance officers are obligated to respectfully refuse the bequest.

A COMPREHENSIVE THEOLOGY OF FINANCE

A pastor's theology of finance should include guidance for individuals, church officers, and trustees (those who usually receive bequests). A pastor's theology of finance, however, is not useful until it is shared and explained. It does not guide people unless they accept and internalize its precepts. Therefore, a pastor's theology must continually be shared and taught through preaching and in small group settings.

It has been demonstrated by some pastors that preaching on a regular basis about the theology of giving and finance produces great awareness among Christians as to how they should handle their personal resources. It has been discovered by many pastors who have preached regularly on finance theology that the benefits of such sermons accrue not only to the listeners but to the pastors as well.

The primary obligation of a pastor is to develop, share, and revise a theology of giving that is broad and strong enough to deal with individual giving, church resources, and bequests. The following chapters will deal with the specifics of securing and handling money. Those chapters must be viewed through the theological lenses serious study of the New Testament can provide.

$

PART 1
Raising Money

A typical pastor will be confronted with raising money for the church budget within the first few months of being sent or called to a parish. In some settings, the need for raising money will be to meet a deficit, to handle a building project, or to purchase property or equipment. There may be intimations of needs during a minister's pre-call interview. When this happens, the new pastor usually has some knowledge of his or her expected role in fund raising.

Unfortunately, many pastors resist taking any role in raising money in the church. They hold to a common assumption among pastors, re-enforced in many seminary settings, that money matters will be handled by lay persons in the parish. This is, and should be, the case. However, organizing and training lay persons so they can deal with money matters in the church effectively and making certain they raise the needed money are ultimately the pastor's responsibilities. The pastor is the only full-time person in most parishes who can organize, train, and put to work a successful fund-raising team.

This does not mean the pastor makes calls on people asking them for money. It does mean the pastor must lead or find a qualified leader (a private consultant, firm, or denominational office) who can guide a congregation through a fund-raising program. Being acquainted with resources and people outside the local church who can assist in fund raising is a necessity. The pastor is in a position either to know such people or have access to individuals who do know competent church fund-raisers.

A second function of a pastor in church fund raising is to be acquainted with the processes used in various types of fund-raising activities. For example, raising money for the annual budget follows a well-defined and clearly described formula and schedule. Adaptations of the formula and schedule are in print and available for the asking. The pastor must understand the basic processes as well as the various types of adaptations that can be made either in scheduling or in applying the formula to different-sized congregations. This knowledge will enable him or her to help lay persons through difficult periods even though another person is doing most of the leading in the fund-raising program.

The pastor does not assume leadership in fund raising just because he or she knows how it is to be done. Yet, the pastor is the on-site person to whom lay leaders look when they are uncertain about scheduling and when they become skeptical about the acceptance of a process by their fellow church members. The pastor who knows the various processes of fund raising, and can offer advice and modifications, will ensure the successful completion of a fund-raising program.

A third function of a pastor is to understand the procedures normally used for capital funds campaigns. The capital funds campaign is usually used to finance a renovation, purchase a building or piece of office or visual aid equipment, to pay off a mortgage, or to reduce or eliminate a substantial debt. A capital funds program assumes that money contributed toward its goal will be in addition to funds given for support of the annual budget. Therefore, a capital funds campaign must convince people who are already giving to give extra money for a specified time while not reducing the amount they normally give to support the annual budget.

PART 1: RAISING MONEY

The pastor, in addition to knowing about people or organizations that can help the congregation design and execute such a campaign, must be aware of the techniques used in this type of fund-raising activity. The process is clearly defined and routinized by those whose business it is to conduct such campaigns. Being aware of these routines and the manner in which contribution estimates are calculated in order to challenge givers is a pastor's responsibility. Knowing the reputation and abilities of various capital fund-raisers is another.

A fourth function of pastors with regard to fund raising is understanding the importance of memorials and endowments, not only to the church but also to church members. Memorials and endowments, given because of a particular church member's life, can be used for missions, building programs, and program expansion in general. Each of these has significance for a church. However, being willing to think of memorials and endowments as ways of bolstering the church's programs is a challenge to many pastors. These types of fund raising demand that a pastor be sensitive to parishioners' desires to memorialize and endow. Discovering these desires may be a direct result of pastoral care, but encouraging and directing their use depend on a pastor's sensitivity to the matter of fund raising.

A recurring opportunity for pastors is to raise money for missions and outreach. It does not take a special kind of pastor to be adept at this type of fund raising. It does demand careful research, use of appropriate promotion materials, securing of audiovisuals, and scheduling of speakers. The techniques of fund raising for missions and outreach will demand of some pastors a renewal of their commitment to the spread of the gospel.

These are topics included in part 1. The discussions describe the techniques and special requirements of each type of fund raising. Additional aids, including denominational officers, are listed under Resources, which follows chapter 11.

Chapter 2

THE CHURCH BUDGET

The most persistent fund-raising need of every congregation is the underwriting of its annual operating budget.
This is not an easy task to accomplish year in and year out.
Yet, when the steps outlined by most successful fund-
raisers (and detailed in the every-member visitation
programs produced by denominations) are followed
carefully, it is not as difficult as it is time-consuming.
Carefully following each step normally produces four
results: (1) realistic church goals, (2) trained lay leaders,
(3) members and constituents who are informed and
excited about the church's program, and (4) enough
money pledged and given to accomplish the goals.

There are three aspects of raising money for the annual
church budget:

(1) planning, which includes goal setting;

(2) promotion and communication of goals, and programs needed to achieve the goals; and

(3) an effective method of collecting money or pledges
or both from members and constituents. Each of these
elements of the fund-raising process is accomplished using
a schedule. The process takes time because it involves
planning, recruiting lay volunteers to assist with various
phases, and perseverance to finish within the agreed upon

schedule. A discussion of each of these elements can help a pastor to understand the procedure and adapt it to the congregation he or she serves.

PLANNING

The first step in raising money for the annual church budget is helping the congregation set realistic program goals. Goal setting involves analyzing one's situation by asking such questions as, What are the church's internal strengths and needs? What are its growth possibilities? What are its community outreach potentials? What are the denominational requirements it must meet, including its money assessments? And, What are the fixed expenses, such as mortgage payments, that must be included in the budget? These are some of the questions a congregation must answer during the goal-setting process.

Answers to these questions about the internal life and external environment of the church will come as the congregation studies itself, its relationship to its community, and its community. This study will be conducted by the church's leaders. Most often, they will use a self-study guide or contract with a consultant who may be a denominational staff member.

A study can provide relatively objective information upon which the church can build its goals for the year. Churches with limited resources or with talented lay persons can write to their denominational research and planning offices for the goal-setting self-study guide. They can follow this guide in conducting their study during the goal-setting process.

A primary need as the church builds realistic goals is accurate data about the church and its environment. Only after such information is available can a church turn its dreams for the future into realistic goals. Following the creation of goals, church leaders and members, through dialogue, further revise goals into workable programs. Let's examine the entire process one step at a time.

CHURCH BUDGET

1. The Church's Internal and External Environment

Every church, about every five years, needs to look at itself and its environment as objectively as possible. Such an analysis helps church members and leaders understand what is taking place within the membership and in the community being served by the church.

Changes tend to sneak up on church leaders. In one congregation, for example, young people were moving away from the church's primary service area in large numbers. This emigration had not been noticed by the church because its program continued to attract people. They commuted to the church during the week in order to participate in those parts of the program they liked. However, the pastor began to notice that the Sunday worship service was beginning to attract mostly older people. The self-study for this congregation pointed to the need to develop goals for a new target group, older neighborhood residents.

Another church was located in a community in which a new housing development had been constructed within a half a mile of its building. Shortly after the development became occupied, church leaders noted a significant increase in the number of younger families who were attending worship and church school. This church had to revise its goals to accommodate increased expenses incurred from training teachers and from the purchase of additional materials for its church school. It discovered, during its study, that many of the young mothers worked outside the home. Consequently, the church pioneered a child-care center in the community.

Most changes in a five-year period are not as dramatic as these two examples, yet changes do occur. People move, die, and are replaced by new residents. With each change, new potentials for program and outreach are created. Within any five-year period, enough change takes place that a church that intends to minister effectively to its members will need to look carefully at its membership as well as its community and service area.

Congregational self-study guides, available from most denominational planning and research offices, contain the following steps for conducting a self-study: (1) collection of census or marketing information about who lives in the area and what changes have taken place in the past few years (census data from the government are for ten-year intervals, but updates from regional governmental agencies or marketing firms can be used to estimate changes); (2) collection and analysis of information from governmental and private planning groups regarding new facilities or services (highways, housing developments, schools, etc.) projected for the area; (3) securing of data about church members so comparisons can be made with census information (age, sex, schooling completed, income, occupation, number of children, marital status, etc.); and (4) instructions for mapping where members live.

This various demographic data provides clues about the members of the church, and when it is compared to census information, church leaders can identify those groups most attracted to, or in need of, the church's program. For example, the primary clientele of a church may be people whose incomes are much lower than the average income of the neighborhood. If the low-income people are community residents, the church discovers its program is attractive to a low socioeconomic group. The congregation may have to decide whether these people will continue to be the focus of its program. If so, the church may need long-term financial assistance from the denomination. Such a congregational decision will require concerted and cooperative attention from denominational officials as well as local church members.

Church leaders, after collecting data through the self-study, will compile a profile of church membership and the community. This profile will give leaders a comparison of current and potential members and an adequate basis upon which to conduct the next step of the planning process, futuring.

2. Futuring

The Christian faith is forward looking. It looks beyond the present to a future in which life is perfect in every way. Of course, that future lies in an eternity unknown to humans. The future for most people most of the time, Christian church leaders and members included, usually is no more than ten years forward. A local church, when it thinks and dreams about the future, limits itself to five or fewer years except when it builds a building. Then, its future is at least as long as the mortgage and, at most, the period of time in which the building will be useful.

The initial phase of futuring is conducted with the official body of the congregation. Each person is asked to envision the church as he or she would like it to be within three years. This is to be summarized in one sentence. These visions are shared with the group and then people are grouped into clusters of threes. These small groups are asked to agree on one future from the three brought to the group by its members. The results are then shared with the large group. The large group is asked to prioritize the kinds of futures it would like based on the items submitted by the clusters of threes. After the items have been prioritized, the top four items are assigned to each of four groups. These groups, made up of the earlier clusters of threes, are asked to create goals, identify data needed to assure the realistic formulation of programs to meet those goals, and schedule the implementation of those goals and their budgets.

The time allotted for the futuring process is at least two and one-half hours but it can be an overnight retreat. The results will be approximately the same except for more discussion and more detail that is available in an overnight retreat.

3. Goal Setting

The futuring process begins with a small, elected group from the congregation. Goal setting demands an expansion and review of the results of the futuring process by many members of the congregation. The goal-setting process seeks to involve as many persons as possible, and so it uses a format that includes individual and group response to the ideas and futures proposed by the futuring group.

The first step in goal setting is to summarize and submit to each organization in the church the results of the futuring process. Each organization is asked to study the goals and to refine them from the perspective of the organization's needs. (If the organization desires, it can engage in a futuring process similar to that used by the official futuring committee of the church.) The new and revised goals are given to the futuring committee for further revision and combination with goals submitted by other organizations.

The futuring committee of the congregation, after revising goals on the basis of feedback from the organizations, may decide it needs additional data from church members. If this happens, it should schedule hearings for other church members. These hearings allow persons who do not belong to organizations, or who were not present at organization meetings in which goals were discussed, to have an opportunity to express their ideas and hopes for the church's potential program. The hearings will include an opportunity for all members of the congregation to have their say.

The data from these hearings will be reviewed and a final set of congregational goals will be created by the futuring committee of the church. The governing body will then approve goals that extend into the future three years; however, the goals will be revised and further extended each year so the church can continue to have a three-year cycle of goals toward which it is working.

This planning process will result in excitement within the

leadership, if not within the entire membership of the congregation. The next step must capture the enthusiasm generated during the futuring and goal-setting steps and direct it so that members will commit money and time to the church's program. This is the promotion and education phase.

PROMOTION AND EDUCATION

Goal setting, no matter how elaborate, is useless until the goals are attached to programs that people can support. Not only must such an attachment be made, but people must also be asked to support the programs with their time and with their money. This is the second phase of money-raising programs for annual church budget support. The general practice followed in promotion and communication of goals and proposed programs for upcoming years is to use letters, charts, and audiovisuals with members during a three- to four-week period. The intent of these promotion and education techniques is to alert people to the relationship between the goal setting in which they have participated and the programs of the church. Ideally, such promotion will help people understand their part in putting into effect the programs that goal setting has pointed to.

Congregational meetings are an important part of this phase of fund raising. One or more dinners are planned during which the church budget is presented and explained. This is an information meeting, the primary outcome of which is that most church members know the extent of the programs supported by their congregation. This is the only way they have of grasping its local involvement as well as its worldwide outreach through missions and denominational activities. In churches that do not communicate through educational and promotional events annually, church members are ignorant of the breadth of their church's programs.

Another form of promotion or communication or both is

for one or more lay persons to explain the goals and budget during worship services. This is generally done as part of the worship experience. The intent is to inform. Sometimes audiovisuals, such as charts and filmstrips, are used to help members visualize activities and programs sponsored by the church.

Such a presentation may include an analysis of what one dollar can do to support the budget. Most of the time, a chart is utilized to diagram giving patterns for the past year. These data are included to elicit thinking and to promote increased giving by members. The comparison charts are generally reserved for a week or two prior to the actual collection of pledges.

COLLECTING PLEDGES

This is the climactic part of annual budget support campaigns. Persons are given pledge cards and asked to commit themselves to a specific amount of financial support for the year through weekly, monthly, quarterly, or annual contributions. In congregations that do not use pledge cards, other means are used to ensure regular income. In most such churches, a personal written commitment is made and kept by the donor.

A variety of techniques for collecting pledges exists. Those deemed most effective involve face-to-face contact with potential donors by visitors who have been trained to make a promotion and education call. These people are trained in calling techniques and must thoroughly understand the budget. After training, each visitor is assigned a list of constituents or church members. The visitors are asked to make their calls within a specified time, usually a week.

Many churches collect pledges from attendees during worship service on pledge day. In these churches, pledging is a part of the service. It is appropriate to use a congregational procession to allow pledgers to put their commitment cards on the altar. The cards become a symbol of church members' intent to dedicate themselves to Christ for the coming year.

Collecting pledge cards through a pony express system is also an effective way of helping people support the annual budget. Under this plan, the parish is divided into sectors with captains assigned to each. On pledge day, the captain brings a pouch in which people can put their pledge cards. The pouch is given to one family, who pledge and then carry it on to the next family, and so forth. The final recipient of the pouch returns it to the captain or calls for the captain to come and pick it up.

Variations of the visitation, collection at worship, and pony express systems of pledge collection can also be used. Their only purpose is to encourage people to sign up to give regularly to the church's budget. After the pledges have been collected, most churches have a dedication service for the cards and the givers.

In some instances, pledges of time are asked for as well as money. Commitments of time are usually related to specific talents or abilities of members. While the budget is clearly defined and money given can be designated to support it, gifts of time are more nebulous. Many congregations have no preconceived means by which to utilize time commitments. It is important, before utilizing talent cards or asking for time commitments, to have enough jobs in the church available for everyone who wants to volunteer. Church members' expectations are raised merely by asking for a time commitment. If there are no jobs to do and a commitment is made, the credibility of the church and its leadership is threatened.

When the three phases of this finance process are used—planning, promotion and education, and a means of securing pledges—a congregation will normally be able to underwrite its budget. The times when it will be unable to do so are those in which the church's community experiences an unexpected change in economic condition (prolonged strike, shutdown of a major industry, etc.) or when church leaders create a budget without considering input from members. Inherently, the process is success oriented.

CAUTIONS AND ALTERNATIVES

An intensive process of planning and training, advocated by most professional fund-raisers, can be successful approximately once in three or four years. The exception occurs in those churches with a staff person who can serve as the leader every year. The procedure is labor intensive and requires much time from such a leader. The main difficulty congregations face who do not have such a leader is not with any part of the process but finding the number of people required to make it work well.

An every-member campaign requires eight to twelve weeks of intensive activity from several people. Finding these people and training them is a major problem in most congregations. It is not a liability when the program is used no more than once in three years, however, since people give large amounts of time to the church for programs few and far between. A yearly program is what can cause job burn-out and is to be pursued gingerly by the pastor, if at all.

Adapting the process to a small church or a church not used to pledging requires professional skills. On the surface it would appear that a pastor could select pieces of the process and create his or her own fund-raising package for a congregation. This does not work in most congregations because of the way the process and supporting literature are designed. A church wanting an intensive program needs to commit itself to the package made available by denominational stewardship offices, or hire a professional to lead.

When a less intense campaign is being considered, a church can and should develop its own schedule and materials. Design the materials on the basis of the three components described above, remembering that professionals feel face-to-face contact will result in the best giving. Remember too that good promotion and effective use of worship during the pledging phase of the process have worked well in many congregations, especially those with small memberships and an informal ambience.

Congregations can benefit greatly from professional leadership in the annual budget fund-raising process. In some communities, smaller congregations combine their leaders and conduct a campaign simultaneously in order to use denominational or professional fund-raisers. These congregations feel the side benefits of trained and informed lay persons, who have a long-term effect on their program efforts. In this way, they are able to justify the cost of hiring professionals.

A major task, often neglected or given a low profile in the process, is following up after pledges have been made. The most effective way to do this is through a quarterly report to pledgers and givers. Every three months, the financial secretary sends a statement to every pledger and giver noting when gifts were made and how those gifts measure up against the original pledge. While many congregations have a financial reporting system like this, relatively few ensure a continuous flow of information to contributors about programs and their execution. Letting people know how well goals are being met is very important to the success of next year's budget finance campaign.

THE PASTOR'S ROLE

The pastor's roles in raising money for the annual budget are part of each stage of the process.

1. The most important pastoral role is helping the church envision a future. It is at this point a pastor injects a theological basis for outreach, for nurture, for worship, for mission, and for community involvement. It is during

futuring that the pastor can help break the parochialism that affects most churches.

2. The pastor's influence on goal setting is critical as well. The tendency of many churches is to maintain the status quo rather than risk embarking in a new direction. The pastor's influence can mean the difference between an enthusiastic congregation and its opposite.

3. The pastor can help a committee decide whether to engage professionals or to use the non-intensive plan described above to design a congregation's approach to budget finance. If the latter course is followed, the pastor will need to function as the professional by helping to develop materials, maintain the schedule, and train people to do their tasks. Most pastors do not have this much time or these types of skills.

4. The pastor's role in collecting pledges is to design the worship experience in such a way that pledges become commitments. The worship experience requires careful thought and ought to be an outgrowth of the time spent by the congregation on the total program.

5. The pastor's role in follow-up will be to try and ensure that people who have volunteered time will be trained and given jobs to do.

It is unthinkable that a congregation can develop its programs and raise money to support them without the involvement of the pastor in every phase of the process. When a pastor looks at the components of a congregation's fund-raising process, that pastor will know what strengths he or she can bring to the process and where another person will be needed. It is the pastor's responsibility to convince congregation leaders to obtain that other assistance.

ONE-TIME SPECIAL REQUESTS

There are occasions when a special need occurs and for which a regular pledge campaign is too cumbersome or is unnecessary. Such an occasion might be due to a unique opportunity to minister in the community, to a breakdown that necessitates repairing a heating or cooling system, or to make a significant contribution to disaster relief. The needs cannot be met within the budget but congregation leaders want to give church members an opportunity to contribute on a one-time basis for this need or event. It is for these occasions that a special one-time fund-raising request is most appropriate.

The one-time request is handled in the following manner. The governing body of the congregation decides the request is necessary to meet an obligation (the church is in a financial crisis) or to rise to a challenge. The board's decision should clearly specify that the money sought is over and above the congregation's regular contribution and that the special request will not be repeated even if the money goal is not reached.

These decisions of the governing body are next conveyed to the congregation and a date on which pledges and contributions will be accepted is set. Members receive, at least a month in advance, materials outlining the need and the decisions of the governing body. The pastor announces it from the pulpit during worship, and lay persons are given a minute to explain the need or outline the opportunity at each worship service for three weeks prior to the collection date. A special worship service of commitment is planned for the day on which money and pledges are to be accepted.

The day arrives and during the worship service people are asked to bring their contribution or pledge or both to the altar. Within the week, people are notified of the amount raised and any alternative plans needed to meet the goal for which the offering was made. In many churches, the careful use of a one-time request is quite effective. As with other fund raising, the amounts collected depend on the effectiveness of the promotion and education that precedes commitment day.

In some places where such requests have been made,

collections have exceeded expectations. A one-time campaign is not to be confused with a capital funds campaign, however. It is for a pressing need that cannot be met in any other way. It should be used with discretion and must be well planned and executed.

SUMMARY

Fund raising for the annual budget is the most common fund-raising need encountered by a pastor. Once in a while the pastor may encourage a congregation to use the one-time special request to meet an obligation or to pay a debt. This special request may be for $10,000 or $2,000,000 depending on the need and the kinds of resources a congregation believes its members have at their disposal. At some point during a career, it will be necessary for a pastor to get involved in a capital funds campaign. While this is similar in many ways to the annual budget fund-raising process, it has some unique features. It is to this special process of fund raising we now turn.

Chapter 3

CAPITAL IMPROVEMENTS

A capital fund-raising campaign in the church is usually for the purchase or renovation of a piece of property such as real estate or equipment. In some instances, a capital funds campaign is conducted to pay off a long-term debt, such as a mortgage. Capital improvement usually involves long-term commitment to the extent that it cannot be adequately financed by one or two annual budgets. Thus, a capital funds campaign will often be necessary for a capital improvement project and will require donations in addition to contributions to regular church budgets.

The need for capital improvement may be decided by nonchurch agencies, such as a building inspector who issues a condemnation or a denial for a particular use of a building. Another situation may occur in which a denominational agency requires renovation of a building as a condition for granting mission aid. In these situations, the church must decide whether to meet the requirements or to curtail its programs. In other situations, church leaders may discover during the planning process a need for facility improvements or debt reduction. Or capital improvements may be initiated by a church that uses a capital plan. The capital plan, seldom developed and followed carefully by individual congregations, focuses on the systematic maintenance and improvement of church assets. The capital plan may include provisions for the purchase of equipment (audiovisual, worship, fixtures, etc.), building renovation, land purchase, or all three.

Capital improvements may be funded through special need campaigns, building and improvement funds to which people can pledge during the annual budget campaign, endowments, and memorials.

THE SPECIAL NEEDS CAMPAIGN

One church in which I served needed a parsonage. The Board of Trustees did not think it was feasible to make such a purchase but they had committed themselves to finding and buying a parsonage within a year of the appointment of a full-time minister. Within a few months, a house became available within a block of the church. It was approved by the Trustees but they did not believe the money could be raised for the down payment. It was time for a special campaign.

How does one go about raising money from members of a congregation who are at or slightly below the average income level? The answer is, the same way one proceeds when people are affluent. The process is the same; it is the dollar figures that are different.

The first step was approval of the purchase by the Trustees. This was followed by approval from denominational officials and committees. It then became necessary to raise the money for the down payment and closing costs. These figures were advertised to the congregation as well as the purpose and total cost of the house.

One evening, with the assistance of one Trustee, the pastor visited half a dozen key lay persons to personally present the opportunity and to ask for their pledge or contribution. Most of the money was raised in this one evening. The next Sunday, the worship service included time during which other members could contribute to the down payment.

The primary concern was for the down payment because mortgage payments were to be included in the annual budget. Thus, this became a special need. This explanation preceded the invitation for contributions at the worship service. That day enough was raised to meet the down payment, the closing costs, and to establish a small balance toward the mortgage.

The process was straightforward. An opportunity arose that had to be acted upon quickly. The appropriate committee in the church made a positive decision and was supported by the denominational officials in charge of property acquisition. The pastor and one Trustee (in other situations it might have been two Trustees or other prominent officials of the congregation) visited a few persons who they thought would be most likely to contribute to this fund. It was hoped that these persons would give at least 80 percent of the amount needed (they did). The remainder was sought during the worship service.

A report of the total amount given and the ways in which the money was spent was given at the worship service the next week. This same report was publicized through the newsletter following the worship service. A celebration of the accomplishment, meeting this special need, was part of worship.

While the special need in this instance was getting enough money together for a down payment for the purchase of a parsonage, the special need in other churches may be for emergency repairs, a past due debt, or supplies to renovate part of a building. The process is the same. The one caution is that special needs should not be a constant part of the fund-raising picture of a church.

CAPITAL IMPROVEMENTS THROUGH A CONTINUING FUND

Some pastors believe a unified budget that includes every fund request for the church is not a healthy way to encourage giving. They insist on separating capital improvements from the regular budget in the form of a building and improvement fund. The theory behind this arrangement is that people should be given an opportunity to contribute more or less to the various activities and needs of the church. Thus, if a person wants to give money to a building fund during the annual budget campaign, the church should accommodate that individual.

This is an especially good theory when applied to capital improvements. People, however, need to know that the Trustees or other responsible committees have a plan for facility maintenance and renovation. A building fund does not generate money unless there is a continuing need. Needs include such items as a mortgage, repainting a sanctuary or church school rooms every three to five years, or purchasing specific equipment. The amount contributed to the building fund will be determined by the needs expressed by those in charge of publicity in the church. If there is no publicity or promotion, the amount contributed will decrease. If there are visible and understood needs, the amount contributed will rise.

Utilizing a continuing building fund should be part of an overall financial plan of the church. This fund should not limit other programs or the community and mission outreach of the congregation, and it won't if the pastor helps members and leaders maintain a capital improvement fund that is consistent with the overall mission plan of the church.

When a congregation decides to separate the current expense budget from the capital improvement budget, the fund-raising procedure is usually combined. The pledge card used in the annual budget finance process will contain two entries, current expense and building fund. People are encouraged to pledge to both. In this way, fund raising for capital improvements becomes part of the annual budget support campaign, which means planning must include capital improvements as well as programs.

ENDOWMENTS

Endowments come as double-edged funds. On the one hand, they make it feasible for a church to do things not possible in any other way. On the other hand, endowments can curtail members' giving merely because they know money is available for the extras a pastor or governing body might propose. When endowment money is used for capital expenses such as painting a building or renovating a room, members get the feeling they do not have to give. Endowment funds are used best as a stimulant for challenging church members to give for a particular capital improvement.

For example, a congregation may need $15,000 to complete a parking lot. Interest income from an endowment may be designated by the Trustees to pay for part of the total cost of the project. The stipulation of the Trustees may be that only $5,000 from the endowment may be used, which means that the congregation must raise the other $10,000 through a capital funds campaign. This method of using endowment income, particularly interest, does not alleviate the congregation's responsibility for giving.

How does a pastor encourage endowments? People endow organizations and programs to extend their personal lives. A pastor may be instrumental in generating endowments by the manner in which he or she ministers. Calling on people, sharing their tragedies and triumphs, and ministering to them in times of crisis are some ways pastors encourage people to give endowments to a church.

Most endowments, however, come to the church because of an individual's or a family's desire to leave a testimony to a particular life or activity. The endowment is in memory of a person's interest in extending the ministry of the church. When this is the reason for endowing a church, the pastor's role should be to guide the use of the gift toward a long-term need or opportunity rather than to allow it to be used for a short-term monument. For instance, a family might want to memorialize a family member by constructing a chapel. If a chapel is not needed, the pastor should try to persuade them to use the money to purchase or construct and maintain a capital improvement that is needed, such as a youth activity building.

Some endowments come in spite of a particular pastor. People give endowments to the church, not to the pastor. Pastors must understand this and be willing to accept rather than resist people's desires to endow. Still, the pastor should make every effort to see that endowments are used in ways that truly benefit the church's programs. If no endowments are forthcoming, however, a pastor must rely on capital funds campaigns for those extras that could be acquired more easily through endowments.

MEMORIALS

Memorials are gifts to the church made in memory of someone and used for a specific purpose. Some churches establish special memorial funds to which people can contribute. These churches have a committee that decides how to spend the money. The Trustees of the fund have a list of items that guides people in their choice of memorial gifts. Contributors are listed in a special book, and the item for which their gift is used is recorded. Often a small plate indicating that the item is "In Memory of _____" is attached.

A memorial gift is made after a death in a family. The pastor, in the normal pastoral care of the family, has a unique opportunity to encourage these gifts because families of church members like to see memorials to their loved ones being used at church. In one congregation, new altar furniture was purchased through a gift in memory of an inactive father by his daughter, who was an active member. In other churches, pianos, paraments, and organs are the result of memorials.

A memorial gift must be for a specific item that is needed

and within the price range of the family to which it is suggested. For example, a young woman in her second year of college was killed in an auto accident. The pastor was called to the family home and helped them work through the immediate realization of death. The family, sometime attenders at worship, told the pastor they did not want large floral bouquets. The pastor, feeling the loss and understanding the family's need to have a token of the girl's life continue, suggested that people be asked to give to a memorial fund at the church in her name. The pastor explained that later the family could discuss in specific terms an appropriate memorial. Meanwhile, only discussion in general about the creation of a special fund was held. This allowed the family and the pastor to concentrate on meeting the crisis of loss.

In another setting a woman's father died of natural causes. The death was expected. A few days after the funeral the pastor visited the woman and suggested it would be fitting for her to consider giving a memorial to the church in her father's name. Nothing specific was discussed, although a range of gifts was described. This range varied in price but was within the circumstances of the woman (most ranges would top at $1,000 and bottom out at $100). The pastor, because the woman was interested in pursuing the conversation, promised to bring a list of possibilities within a week.

In such a case, the pastor could discuss capital needs with the Trustees or could present a list of items to them that could be purchased with the woman's memorial monies. If they approved the list, the pastor could get specific prices and present one or two possibilities to the woman or give her the entire list so she could choose what she wanted to give. The list might include office equipment, stained glass windows, musical instruments, choir robes, hymnals, furniture, or room renovations. Once the woman decided on a memorial, the money would travel through a memorial fund or through the Trustees. A dedication would be held and a plaque affixed to the item. The gift would be recorded in the congregation's book of permanent memorials.

The pastor is the key actor in raising money through memorials. Sensitivity is important but equally imperative is being alert to the needs people have to perpetuate the memory of loved ones. This is done in tangible ways. It is the pastor's responsibility to encourage such giving and to direct it so that people do not become overly elaborate or designate a gift that is not useful to the church's programs.

THE CAPITAL FUNDS CAMPAIGN

An examination of the elements of a capital funds campaign will illustrate the similarity, as well as the major differences, between it and raising money for the annual budget.

Planning for the annual budget often identifies needs that have to be handled by a capital funds campaign. For example, a church may decide to expand its community outreach in the form of a soup kitchen. In order to meet public health requirements, the church discovers it must upgrade its kitchen facilities, its serving area, and its rest rooms. The church, after discovering these needs, affirms its desire to proceed with this ministry. Yet, it must have $23,000 in building improvements within the next four months. Church leaders decide to raise the money through a capital funds drive.

The first phase, following the planning decision and reaffirmation of the church's commitment to the program, is to create information and promotion materials. These materials must be created and produced by the church. The promotion is item specific (renovation of kitchen, serving area, and rest rooms) and is for a designated program (soup kitchen). Even though a professional firm may be asked to lead the campaign, the promotional and educational materials are the responsibilities of the local church.

CAPITAL IMPROVEMENTS

The second phase separates the annual budget from the capital funds campaign. This includes identifying persons who have the potential to make large one-time gifts. These individuals will be selected on the basis of their personal histories as well as their possible interest in the program in question. (In some instances, an individual who does not contribute to the annual budget may be asked for a possible gift to a capital improvement project.) No one is overlooked as the list is created.

The list is created by the financial secretary, the stewardship chairperson, the treasurer, and a couple of other individuals. The pastor may be included in this group. Most of the time, the pastor will be asked for information about certain people because of his or her acquaintance with them through visitation. In any case, the pastor, at some point in the creation of the big-givers list, will have significant input. Without the pastor's input, the capital funds campaign's second phase will not have the breadth of information about members necessary to make it successful.

In the third phase, commitments are secured from the planning group, that is, from those most anxious for the soup kitchen to be established. Then a small group of the Trustees visits each person on the big-givers list. This visitation should produce between 60 and 80 percent of the money needed for the project. The money should be in gifts now or pledges to pay within three months.

The fourth phase is to tabulate the amount secured from the big givers and let members know how much has been secured and how much is still needed. The members are given an opportunity the next Sunday at worship to add their contributions or pledges to this project. The worship service is planned as a time of commitment, and money is given as a special offering, usually by procession to the altar of those contributing.

The fifth phase is to let the people know how much has been collected, what it is being used for, and, if monies collected fell short of or exceeded the mark, how the remainder is to be collected or how the extra is to be used.

SUMMARY

Raising money for capital improvements can be done through special campaigns, establishing a continuing fund for capital improvements to which people may pledge during the annual budget money-raising campaign, directing endowments to capital needs, and soliciting memorials. Each of these tasks involves the pastor in each phase—in planning, promotion, solicitation, and dedication. Knowing the difference between a capital fund campaign and the process used for funding the annual budget, which requires a long-term commitment in the church's program, is critical. Of particular importance is the pastor's role in assisting in the development of the big-givers list. Buildings are very important to ministry since they house and symbolize a congregation. Equally important is the mission outreach of a church. The pastor's important role in raising money for capital improvements becomes even more important in raising money for missions and outreach, as we shall see in the next chapter.

Chapter 4

MISSIONS AND OUTREACH

The church is a worldwide organization, but it depends upon people in individual congregations for financial support. Such people, by giving to missions, are able to witness to, nurture, and care for others who live in different places. Although a missions class may study most often about another country, the church has missions in urban and rural locations within a few miles of most individual churches around the world. Learning about those missions is important if a pastor is attempting to raise money for missions.

The variety of mission activities undertaken by the church makes raising money for their support relatively easy as long as the pastor is committed to the concept of witnessing through missions. A pastor, as in every other phase of fund raising in the church, is the key figure in helping people understand the need and presenting the opportunities for giving to missions.

The pastor has the task of educating and motivating members to contribute to missions. The pastor, however, has access to a bank of resources including explanatory, interpretive, and promotional literature, films and video cassettes, and people. Any one or a combination of these resources can be used to promote the church's mission work.

The availability of resources, however, does not mean each pastor will take advantage of them. Only those pastors who believe the church, through missions, must witness to and serve other people, primarily those who do not support the church and who may be alienated from society as well, will use any of the interpretive resources available to encourage people to support missions.

Literature that explains and promotes a denomination's mission work is usually free. A pastor can order enough of several types of printed materials describing a particular type of mission work, such as medical missions, or work in a specific area, such as Africa, to insert them in worship bulletins or in newsletters being sent to members and constituents. Free interpretive and promotional materials are sent to pastors regularly, usually quarterly.

Mission activity, especially special emphases, is also explained and promoted in articles in denominational magazines or newspapers. Also, pastors can learn of these emphases at mission meetings or at regional denomination meetings. During some of these meetings, personnel from the mission board, or missionaries on leave, may be resource leaders.

Films about specific mission activities are produced by several different denominations. These films deal with these denominations' activities in a given area. The films are usually kept in film libraries by the conference or synod of these denominations. New films and filmstrips are announced through conference newsletters, or promotional fliers about them are included in the conference or synod monthly mailings to pastors.

In some denominational regional meetings devoted to interpreting missions, opportunities for attendees to screen films or filmstrips may be part of the program. Leaders in workshops that discuss specific mission work will show film clips or a film for viewing by pastors and lay persons.

Audio and video cassettes, quite useful in promoting

mission support, are described in conference or denominational promotional literature sent to pastors. These cassettes are usually made available through the conference or synod audiovisual library. Such cassettes, as well as films, are also available for loan from the denominational audiovisual library. A telephone call to either the conference or denominational audiovisual library will tell a pastor in need of a cassette on any given mission topic when it can be sent to his or her congregation.

Promotion of missions, in some denominations, is part of a national agency's job. A pastor can call this agency for information about promotional and interpretive materials on any of the denomination's mission activities. Usually, such an agency has free literature but no films to send to a church.

The abundance of promotional and interpretive materials from the denomination should make raising money for missions easier than other types of fund raising. The pastor who allows denominational agencies to help with promotion and interpretation by using the materials they produce will have an easier job than pastors who do not. Also, using an audiovisual library is important for mission promotion. Promoting through film or video cassette will simplify a pastor's fund raising for missions. A pastor who uses these materials will discover that they increase the willingness of members to contribute to missions. It is up to the pastor, however, to learn about these materials and to make certain they are ordered and used in a congregation.

In addition to free literature and audiovisual resources, three types of links with mission activities can make missions a challenging opportunity for an individual congregation. These links include supporting an individual missionary, joining a local or regional outreach program, and working with a sister church in missions. Examining each of these can aid a pastor in deciding how best to link a church to mission opportunities.

INDIVIDUAL MISSIONARIES

"Be personal" is one of the primary instructions a professional gives to a neophyte fund-raiser. "If people know you have their name in mind, they get the impression that you care about them. In fact, you do care enough about them to learn their names, which also implies that you can combine other facts about them with their names."

Let's assume most pastors are not experienced fund-raisers. The professional's advice to be personal in order to raise money can be an important axiom in raising money for missions in a congregation. The axiom suggests that when a congregation attempts to raise money for missions, it and a missionary, or several missionaries, ought to find ways to be on "personal" terms with each other.

How to be personal with someone one has never met is a problem, but it can be overcome. The first step is to decide what type of mission activity is most important to one's church. The next step is to send a request to the mission board for the names of one or several missionaries whose profiles and activities can be shared with members of the church. A denomination can provide a church with the names and addresses of its missionaries as well as give a brief sketch of their activities.

These two steps start the personalization process because they give the congregation the names of one or several individuals to whom they can address questions and from whom a newsletter may be received. This initial stage of acquaintance makes missions come alive for many people in the congregation because they learn that missions are the result of the work of people.

In larger congregations, it is important to select two or three types of mission activities (medical, education, church) and request the name of a missionary engaged in each type of activity. Such diversification recognizes the variety of interests church members have and project onto mission programs. Being able to put a name with a type of activity helps a church become more active and interested in mission support.

A more involved method of personalizing mission support is for a congregation to assume full or partial financial support of one or more missionaries. This requires an agreement between the church and the missionary, usually through a denominational mission board or agency. The church agrees to pay all or part of the cost of sending a missionary to a particular place for a specific period of time. For example, a church may wish to support a medical doctor in a mission hospital in the Philippines for six months. The church should ask the denominational mission board for the name of such a person and discuss with a representative of the board the process of supporting a missionary for such a period of time.

The mission board will supply names of one or more missionaries and a sketch of each missionary's work as well as personal information about each individual. The church will choose one of them. After the church has made a choice, the mission board, through a representative, will tell the congregation how best to fund the missionary. Usually, money for the support of a missionary is sent through a denominational board or agency. The board notifies the missionary that this specific church is sponsoring him or her for a specific time.

When the first gift is received, the tie between the church and the missionary is established. This beginning may result in a long-distance and long-term relationship. Even if the relationship is short-term it generates interest in mission work of a kind that the church will find in accord with its ministry.

A missionary need not be working in another country to be personally known or supported or both by a church. He or she may be assigned to a church in an urban or rural community within commuting distance of a sponsoring church. For instance, a church in a city neighborhood may ask the denomination to supply a neighborhood worker who can develop a program for young people for after school hours and weekends. This is done through the mission board of the denomination. Any individual church, in that city or from any other place, can help support this missionary. Again, interest in missions is increased because a local church can connect a name and location with the word *mission.*

Raising money to support an individual missionary is made easier when regular correspondence is received and posted. This means the local church must write to its missionary regularly. It means, as well, that letters received from the missionary need to be excerpted and put in the newsletter, quotations excerpted for the bulletin, and the entire letter posted on the bulletin board outside the church office. Making certain letters are written and that those received are posted are tasks usually assigned to a mission committee.

It may be possible to have the individual missionary, supported or adopted as a pen pal by a congregation, speak at the worship service or to a group in the church on occasion. Personal appearances by a missionary increase interest. If a special collection for the missionary's work is taken during the appearance, financial support is increased.

Missionaries are assigned to speak in churches on a regular basis in most denominations. The mission board will notify congregations of times it expects a missionary to be available for speaking in their areas. When a congregation supports a missionary, special arrangements may be made to have the missionary appear once or twice in the church during a time when he or she is in the United States. Scheduling a missionary for appearances in congregations is the responsibility of the mission board through its regional representatives.

It is important that a missionary who is supported by a congregation communicate often with that congregation. The missionary should try to appear personally in the church whenever it is feasible. Being personal is the keynote in missions, and this is reciprocally true of the missionary as well. Fund raising for individual missionaries can be relatively easy when the admonition to "be personal" is observed both by the church and the missionary.

LOCAL AND REGIONAL OUTREACH PROGRAMS

A distinction is made here between *mission* and *outreach* even though some people use the terms interchangeably. The difference between them is how and where they originate.

An outreach program is conceived, initiated, supported, and perpetuated as an activity of one or more congregations in a given area. Most often this program seeks to solve a local issue or to deal with a problem that the church perceives, or churches perceive, to be localized. Outreach does not require great sums of money but can be done with volunteers and the financial resources of one congregation.

For example, one type of outreach program may be a food pantry for persons in an urban neighborhood or near a rural congregation. The problem, need for food to feed families, is local: "These are our neighbors." And the solution is worked out by the members of a church: "We have to take the initiative. After all, we call ourselves Christians."

A regional outreach program may be longer-term and be designed to serve a larger constituency during an especially bad time. For example, a group of churches in one part of a county may band together to collect clothing and food for people who have been flooded out of their homes or who have lost their homes to fire. The rationale for getting involved is the same as for a single congregation—the need is there and the church should help meet it. These needs are perceived to be manageable problems at which the congregations involved can direct their attention and interest. This combination of needs and perceptions makes raising money relatively easy over the short term.

Raising money for outreach programs is not easy, but it is easier when a need is localized. Church members know who the people in need are and realize that their needs are real. It helps to be personal in raising money for outreach as well. For instance, a person who is a recipient of food from a food pantry might be willing to address the congregation. The focus of this talk could be on how the church fills the gap between what various welfare agencies do and what needs to be done in times of hardship. A presentation by such a recipient should not be made as a condition for the church's helping him or her, nor should it compromise the individual's stature or self-image.

It is more difficult to raise money for the continued support of long-term programs. The difficulty arises because supporters begin to characterize recipients as unwilling to help themselves. It becomes the pastor's task to challenge the myth of self-help through factual presentations of conditions. It is important for the pastor to be evenhanded in such presentations, however, because sometimes recipients do use their former plight as an excuse not to do more for their own betterment.

Local outreach programs must be authorized each year in the goal development process of the congregation. This brings the rationale for their support to the attention of the congregation at budget building time. Usually, members are asked to support these programs through the annual budget. When a special need is to be confronted or an emergency arises, a pastor must use one of the fund-raising processes for special needs, outlined earlier.

SISTER CHURCHES

Outreach becomes quite personal when churches decide to become sister churches. The two congregations making this decision may be in totally different settings or they may be across the street from each other. The distinction between them is that they serve different types of members. In uniting, their desire is to expand their understanding of their mission. Their intent is that each learn about and be involved in the life of the other. Of course, being involved in each other's life does not mean everything is done together, nor does it suggest control over the program by one or the other of the churches. The relationship is based on specific activities that supplement the normal program of each church.

For example, a suburban church and an inner city congregation, after an exploration of the idea by the pastors and church leaders, agreed to become sister churches. After study by a combined group of leaders, they agreed that volunteers from the suburban church would work with teenagers in the inner city in an intensive enrichment program, while leaders from the inner city church were to lead adult discussion groups at the suburban church about life and work in a strictly urban environment.

The suburban church recruited and trained one set of volunteers, who spent a year tutoring high school students who needed individual assistance with reading and math, another set, who helped a dozen teenage boys learn how to repair televisions and radios, and a third set, who conducted classes on health and hygiene. The inner city church recruited volunteers who spent one evening a week for a year teaching adult and youth groups about the political realities of getting things done in the city, how groups must organize to force change on city government, businesses, and landlords, and describing some techniques inner city churches use to motivate people who have no goals in life.

The program was supported financially by the suburban church as part of its outreach budget. Money was raised to cover travel expenses for inner city volunteers to come to the suburban church, for materials that were needed in training the teenage boys to fix televisions and radios, and to subsidize trips organized by inner city church members for suburban church members. The costs were not great, but some money was still necessary.

The hardest part of raising this money was helping the governing body in each church adopt the goal of finding and working with a sister church. Once the idea of working with a sister church became a goal, the anticipated costs were included by the suburban church in its annual budget. Both churches were obligated to recruit volunteers. Explaining the venture to each congregation included having people from each church come and talk to the other about their expectations and excitement.

This type of connection between churches is possible even when great distances separate congregations. For instance, a church in the Midwest became a sister congregation with an African church. The intent of the midwestern church was to learn about life in this African community, to give money to help that church secure materials for Christian education, and to send its pastor to continuing education workshops. This particular cooperative venture continued for several years and was productive for both churches.

After the first year, raising money was relatively simple. This was due in part to regular communication through letters, which as noted earlier is very important to fund raising. Another reason was that a member of the midwestern congregation was able to visit the African church and brought firsthand greetings to its members. The pictures and descriptions brought back by the visitor to the midwestern church increased its interest and enthusiasm.

Giving to a sister church is a form of personalizing mission and outreach ministries. As in other cases of personal ministry, raising money is relatively simple because the contributor comes to know the recipient. Letters are a type of feedback that can be used to inspire contributors.

GOING BEYOND EXPECTATIONS

The world is full of need, and the church can meet some of those needs. It cannot meet them all, but if members would become serious about their calling to minister to those without food, shelter, or clothing, many people who exist in deprived situations could find a new life. In order to minister effectively, however, the church must expect more from its people than it has in the past.

The church must survive on a budget that assumes risks rather than on a conservative one. Faith is built on expectations about one's relationship with God. When people are called to express their faith, that calling should be more than a whisper. No congregation should be content to meet a denominational goal for missions and outreach. Every congregation has within sight and sound of its building people in need, and members should contribute to programs that will minister to them.

Natural disasters give rise to special needs. People who have been traumatized through loss need not only money and supplies but ministers. Every church ought to collect special funds for disaster relief annually, if not quarterly. Also, church people need to be trained to minister to each other. Then, if a disaster or need occurs, they will be equipped to fulfill their calling as Christians.

The pastor's responsibility in helping a congregation exceed its own expectations is to inspire and educate the membership. People are willing to give if they see a need. It is up to the pastor to identify those needs that a church can help meet, whether the needs be in the neighborhood, county, nation, or world. Responsibility for raising the level of giving for missions and outreach, therefore, lies with the pastor.

Those pastors willing to become excited about missions and outreach bring new life to their churches. Their challenge offers members an opportunity to make tangible contributions, both in time and money. What is amazing to many pastors who ask is the large number of people who can be inspired to give these gifts.

SUMMARY

Giving to missions and outreach is increased when individual missionaries are supported and separate churches become sisters. Outreach programs focusing on a specific need in a local area are another way to personalize missions. Raising money for personalized missions is relatively easy if letters and pictures are sent regularly and personal visits are made when possible. The pastor is a key individual in mission fund raising because he or she has access to denominational resources that can assist in promotion and interpretation. It is up to the pastor, also, to help church members think big about and give generously to missions.

$

PART 2
Financial Planning

"Exactly what is financial planning? Does it assume I have money left to invest after meeting my obligations? When should I start planning my finances? And once I have a plan, how often should I change it?"

"Those are good questions. Our best strategy is to start where you are now and focus on your immediate and long-range goals."

"I don't understand. You want to know my life goals? I thought we were dealing with finances."

"We are. But I can't help you until I know what you intend to be or would like to be five, ten, or twenty years from now."

Financial planning is long-range planning and focuses on the use of money to help meet some of a person's long-term goals. Financial security at retirement, purchasing a home or property or appliances, saving money to put children through school or to finance a vacation or study leave, or putting aside money in order to meet unforeseen emergencies are some of the objectives of financial planning. The purpose of such planning is part of the goal system of an individual or a family.

Financial planning is needed by everyone, especially those who feel they do not have enough money or income to worry about planning. In fact, planning spending, saving, and giving often is more important to those who have low incomes than it is for people with high incomes because of the lack of resource flexibility available to people with low incomes. For example, getting and using credit to advantage is more difficult for people with low incomes than it is for people with medium to high incomes. For low income people, credit is often a necessity and a burden, while for high income people the use of credit affords one form of tax relief. Using income and money resources well is the primary aim, as well as a result, of good financial planning.

Age is a factor in financial planning only in terms of the length and kinds of life goals a person sets. Young adults and senior citizens need to plan their finances carefully even though the length of time they have to accomplish their goals is vastly different. People in their thirties need to plan finances to cope with the extensive expenses of the forties, while people in their fifties must plan for retirement. The point of financial planning is to make certain that the financial resources a person or family has available at any age can be used to accomplish the primary goals of that person or family.

The techniques of financial planning are familiar to most people. These include listing income, obligations, assets, and liabilities. Once these have been listed, the task of working out a procedure for accomplishing specific financial goals, such as reducing one's debt burden or establishing a meaningful savings plan, is undertaken. This task may involve an individual who functions as a financial planner. This individual can assist a person or family to analyze income, assets, obligations, liabilities, and goals in order to work out realistic spending patterns. In this entire process, the most difficult task is creating long-range goals for one's life. The second hardest part of financial planning is disciplining oneself to create and follow a plan. It is for these two elements in financial planning that experts are hired most often.

The church does not like to believe it should be involved

in financial planning since this is for individuals and families. The church, however, does not hesitate to speak about morals, values, and social vice, and the use of money is after all a stewardship and values issue. If the church speaks to either of these, it should address and create plans for helping people with financial planning. How this is done and for whom the programs are conducted are questions of strategy that must be answered during church goal-setting processes.

Financial planning is an important task for individuals, families, and the church. The pastor's role in this comes from within the church's program. However, it is beneficial for most pastors to know the elements of, and the need for, financial planning for their own personal lives and for those with whom they counsel.

The next two chapters discuss financial planning from different perspectives. Chapter 5 describes the basics of financial planning and includes "how-to" as well as "for-whom" discussions. Chapter 6 deals with financial planning as a church program.

Chapter 5

BASICS
OF FINANCIAL PLANNING

An aura of high finance surrounds the idea of financial planning. The aura is misleading because financial planning does not require that an individual or family have a lot of money. Financial planning is helpful to everyone, especially those with limited incomes and those who have many financial obligations, because it allows them to better allocate their resources. Effective financial planning demands a willingness to look carefully at one's financial situation and a desire to plan how to use one's income and assets to best advantage.

Financial planning deals with one's income, debts, assets, and long-term obligations. Consequently, it must be entered into with honesty and self-discipline.

Honesty is a prerequisite of good financial planning. Fudging on figures or disregarding seemingly minor financial obligations will result in skewed and unreliable data. For example, in listing income and expenses for a month, a person may be tempted to add an extra $100 because the regular monthly income looks skimpy. This extra $100 may come only two or three times a year, as a gift, a bonus, or overtime pay. Therefore, the projections based on the inaccurate income figures will be $900 to

$1,000 too high. For some people, this amount of money represents an appliance, a savings account, or the down payment for an auto.

Anyone who has attempted to live by a budget understands self-discipline. Personal financial resources are finite with a beginning and an ending. People create budgets to allocate finite financial resources in order to have a life pattern that is relatively secure and pleasant. When a person who has established a budget begins to overspend and to disregard the amounts allotted to various types of expenses, the result can be financial chaos. In some instances, disregarding a budget can result in living on the edge of financial disaster.

Two young people illustrate the difference between living by a budget and living in spite of a budget. A young woman with her first job set up a budget based on her monthly income, that is, her actual take-home money. She was quite careful about keeping within her guidelines for each type of expense. Within five years she had a good savings account, modest investments, and a comfortable life-style.

A second young woman beginning her first job figured she had enough money to do some splurging with each paycheck. She bought a luxury every two weeks and used a charge card to pay for the items. At the end of three months, she was up to the credit limit on her card, with most of her income going to pay for the good times she had had. She had barely enough money left to pay for the necessities of food, clothing, and shelter.

The difference between these two young women's financial situations is based on careful planning and adhering to the plan, and doing the opposite. Money must be used carefully and with self-discipline. Financial resources are limited. However, people with the same amounts of money available each month can have quite different life-styles. The primary reason for these differences often can be traced to discipline and planning for the use of money.

BASICS OF FINANCIAL PLANNING

Decisions about how to use money become difficult when the choice is between an immediate necessity and a needed item that may be deferred for a short time. Decisions are equally hard when legitimate objectives can be met with the same amount of money. For instance, a person may ask, "Which should I do, add a few dollars to my loan payment this month or get a new suit?" Both alternatives are good. The choice must be based on which alternative better helps move the person toward specific life goals.

Three characteristics—honesty, self-discipline, and the ability to make and abide by hard decisions—are prerequisites of an excellent financial plan. People are not robots, and emotion plays a large part in life, especially when finances are involved. Everyone cannot be totally disciplined or willing to make hard decisions all the time. Thus, an acceptable, as compared to an excellent, financial plan will be achieved by most people who are willing to commit themselves to discipline, honesty, and hard decisions much of the time. A pastor can help people understand the need for financial planning by assuring them that it is acceptable to have occasional spending excesses and disregard disciplined financial planning for a while.

A financial plan is exactly that, a plan. It can be altered, disregarded, or changed completely. It is desirable as a blueprint for a particular life pattern. If that life pattern changes or becomes too oppressive and restrictive, it and the financial plan must be altered. A pastor can relieve much tension by explaining to people the need to continually evaluate and update their financial plans.

A pastor should also discuss the merits and liabilities of financial planning in the context of life planning. Examining life goals from a Christian perspective can be done through sermons or in small group presentations. These discussions need not be specifically related to financial planning, although talking about life goals in a stewardship context is a proper method for beginning a presentation on financial planning.

Financial planning occurs against a background of life goals. These are ultimates toward which individuals and families work for an entire lifetime. Life goals set the context for a discussion about basic elements of financial planning.

ELEMENTS OF FINANCIAL PLANNING

Financial planning for most church members consists of establishing a method for using money that provides them with what they need and some of what they want while keeping them financially solvent. This rather simplistically stated goal must be achieved in a complex and demanding environment that makes the rational use of money resources very difficult. Financial planning becomes more complicated when an individual wants the plan to include tax advantages and tax shelters. In such a case, the person needs to consult a tax lawyer. Most church members develop a financial plan without the complication of tax shelters.

A life goal, the foundation for financial planning, influences events for a long time. For example, a family with two children may decide those children should have a college education. This emphasis, when followed for a long time, becomes a life goal. When parents decide quite early in a child's life to provide the child with a college education, some changes will be necessary in the family's financial planning, but not to any large and significant degree in spending habits. However, if the decision to send children to college is not made until the children are sophomores or juniors in high school, immediate and significant adjustments may need to occur in the family's use of money. These changes may dictate that the family do without vacations for eight years and that no new automobile be purchased for eight years.

BASICS OF FINANCIAL PLANNING

The life goal of the parents is to emphasize education, one aspect of which is providing a college education for the children. In order to achieve this goal, the family must plan their finances. Financial planning, in this family, calls for adjusting their use of money resources so that this life goal may be achieved. This illustration points to the first element of financial planning, setting goals. Two types of goals—life goals and short-term goals—are needed in financial planning.

1. Life Goals

The most basic element in personal and family planning, as this illustration indicates, is to create, to enunciate, or to surface, life goals. Some people will not have a clear set of life goals because they have never thought about them. This is particularly the case with younger people. Other persons have life goals but have not stated them clearly. These individuals live by intuition or feeling. They can state their goals if pressed. Another group of people lives with subterranean goals. Their beliefs and ideas about life are far below their consciousness. With great effort, they can surface these beliefs and weave them into a set of life goals.

A financial plan should extend through one's expected lifetime. A lifetime perspective helps people think beyond both the depressions and high points, which are part of life. Every person's life will include peaks and valleys, with the number of dollars available changing according to work situations, life settings such as marriage and children, investments, and unexpected obligations. Effective financial planning occurs when a person's or a family's long-term goals remain the same in spite of high or low points in income. By their very nature, life goals take a lifetime to achieve.

Life goals are the basis of ambitions and dreams. They can influence people without ever being acknowledged. In order to create an effective financial plan, people must recognize their life goals. They can be encouraged to do this by stating what they hope to accomplish in life. This statement will identify some of the forces working within them to create their desires and ambitions. These forces are unrecognized life goals.

A list of three to five life goals will encompass what is important to most people. If the list grows much longer, the individual needs to prioritize the goals in order to focus on two or three. People cannot effectively meet more than two or three life goals in a lifetime.

2. Short-Term Goals

The second element in personal and family planning is to create short-term goals consistent with one's life goals and which, over the long haul, will accomplish the life goals. For instance, a person might state a life goal of having a house that can become a focus of family life. This individual recognizes that achieving such a goal is a long way down the road and to get there will require sequential short-term goals. One short-term goal will be to save a certain percentage of regular income for several years in order to have money for a down payment on a house. When enough money has been accumulated for a down payment, the next short-term goal will be to find and purchase the house.

Other short-term goals will include learning what to look for in a house and deciding on its setting and location. Once these goals have been met, it will be possible to find just the house one can purchase. Then, it may be necessary to find work in the area in which the prospective house is located or to become acquainted with and establish accounts in one or more banks in the area. The next step in achieving the life goal is to make the house a home, which requires a lot of living and loving by the people who live in it.

The sequence of short-term goals in this illustration takes several years to achieve but it has a design and a purpose. A life goal is accomplished by creating and achieving short-term goals. Because of their long-term nature, life goals are met in stages. Each stage through which one progresses in achieving a life goal involves financial planning.

KNOWLEDGE OF ONE'S FINANCIAL BASE

It is surprising to meet people who have not calculated what they make and spend monthly. They may know how much they make an hour or a week but have not sat down to figure out their regular monthly income and outgo. They have no budget and compute their taxes by using the short form.

It is essential for a person to know about income and expenses as well as assets and liabilities in order to begin creating a financial plan. Income is the amount a person has after taxes have been deducted from the paycheck. Expenses include every obligation a person has that must be paid for in money. Assets are those things a person owns. An automobile, a house, a bicycle, stocks, bonds, money in savings accounts, and items that can be resold are examples of assets. An asset has a value, which is determined by how much a person will receive if it is resold or, in the case of bonds, when they are redeemed for money. An old family picture is not an asset because it has no commercial value even though its emotional value is great for family members. Liabilities are unpaid debts. Included in this list are charge card balances, mortgages, loans, department store charges, oil company charges, and similar obligations. These tend to be divided into current and long-term with the distinction being determined by the type of product, service, or item for which the liability was incurred. For example, a mortgage and an automobile loan may be long-term because both extend beyond three years, whereas the balance of a charge card is immediate because it has a due date of this month.

A fifth item to be included in a person's knowledge of his

or her financial base is insurance. The different types of insurance include life, casualty, loan, and investment. Life insurance is purchased to offset lost income and to meet immediate and long-term liabilities if one of the breadwinners dies. For example, mortgage insurance is acquired to pay off the balance of a mortgage if a person dies. Casualty insurance is to protect assets either fully owned or in the process of being purchased, such as a house or an auto, should some disaster strike. Loan insurance is acquired to pay off an existing loan in case something happens to make it impossible for an individual to work any longer. Investment insurance is a special form of insurance. It is the same as a savings plan in that it can be cashed in at a particular time. This type of insurance is often used to help meet college expenses for children.

A person must accumulate the information from personal records about each of these five items prior to beginning financial planning. This information becomes the foundation upon which a financial plan will be constructed.

The objective of financial planning is to create and maintain a surplus of income so that assets will be cumulative. Liabilities are incurred in order to meet certain personal and family needs but, whenever possible, are engaged upon in such a manner that they add to assets or support the life-style for which the financial plan is created. Insurance is purchased to protect the family assets and to offset the possibility of increasing its liabilities in case of mishap or death.

HOW TO CREATE A FINANCIAL PLAN

A financial plan is based on annual income and expenses but must be adjusted to a monthly basis for most people. This allows them to deal with amounts of money they better understand because these amounts are on check stubs and bank balances.

BASICS OF FINANCIAL PLANNING

1. Budgeting

The first step in creating a financial plan is to establish an individual or a family budget. The budget is a blueprint for spending, saving, and investing. It allows a person or a family to control expenses and to use income for living style, building up assets, savings, and giving. Of course, it is essential to follow the budget once it is created. The elements in the budget must include income, expenses, saving, giving, and investments.

The discipline of setting up a budget requires a person or family to make a list of liabilities and money income on a monthly basis. The budget juxtaposes these amounts so that income will not be exceeded by expenses. For instance, an individual who makes $300 per week and has liabilities of $280 per week will create a monthly budget with income of $1,200 and expenses totaling $1,120 (even though some bills such as property tax may accrue quarterly). A budget must be based on actual figures or percentages from the last year.

The budget will designate how much money will be spent, or allocated, for each individual and household expense such as food, medicine, utilities, clothing, etc. In addition to spending, the budget will set aside money for discretionary spending such as a box of candy or flowers or whatever. Some people call this their emotion account. Another category of the budget will be for financial contributions to organizations, including the church. An item in some people's budget is for insurance, including auto, household, health, and life. A final category, sometimes ignored, is for savings and investment. This category must be included and kept intact in spite of hard financial times. This budget, with an income side and an expense side that includes at least four major categories, is the base for a financial plan.

2. Building Assets

The next step in financial planning is setting up a list and conducting an analysis of one's personal or family assets and liabilities. The procedure for accomplishing this is similar to completing the assets and liability section of a loan application form. As with a loan, it is important not to overlook any liability, even those that may be considered to be insignificant.

Assets ought to be separated into wholly owned and partially owned. The wholly owned asset, such as a stock, a house, or an appliance, is not encumbered by any liability. For example, a house that is fully owned by an individual is in a different category than a house on which a person is making monthly payments on a mortgage. In this latter situation, a monthly liability is met that increases the amount of equity, or asset, in the house. The difference between building assets and maintaining assets is exemplified by the difference between a wholly owned and partially owned asset.

Assets are accumulated as a part of the budget. They are increased by regular savings from the monthly income or through periodic investments. Purchasing a home is an investment as much as is buying a stock. Each month, a house increases its equity value by the amount paid on the principal of the mortgage as well as by the increase in potential purchase price if a person must sell it. Savings funds may be short-term or long-term when a certificate is purchased. Savings, investments, and purchasing real estate can have roles in building up the assets of a family or an individual.

3. Insurance

The third step of a financial plan is the judicious purchase of insurance. These purchases are made to protect assets and income if a person becomes disabled or dies. Excessive insurance tends to be a waste of money. Insurance is excessive when its costs are such a strain on the budget that the benefits in the long term are jeopardized by short-term costs.

After these three steps have been taken, the financial plan is in place and ready to put into practice. The next step is to test and then to implement the financial plan.

TESTING AND IMPLEMENTING A FINANCIAL PLAN

A financial plan is an idea on paper until it is put into practice. However, it is sound planning to test and revise the financial plan after it has been implemented. The test provides an experience base upon which to make adjustments.

1. The first step in testing a financial plan is to establish a financial goal for the year or half year based on the newly created budget. The goal might be to save a certain amount, to eliminate one or two bills, to save for a special vacation, or to accumulate money to purchase an appliance or an automobile. The goal must be realistic and within the bounds of available cash. Trying to reach this goal will test the budget one has established.

2. Test the plan for six months to a year. If the plan seems to fit one's life-style, set up longer-term goals that are consistent with one's life goals. The discipline learned during the test will enable one to meet the longer-term goals.

3. Annual evaluations are essential. The evaluation will question the percentages used for each major category. When the discrepancy between the budget and reality becomes too large, adjustments in the budget will be made. In addition, attention will focus on the amount of return one is receiving from each type of investment. The result may be the suggestion to change investment policies. If this occurs, information from a broker or a banker as to rates and options for investing will be helpful.

Thus, the steps for creating a financial plan are: setting life goals, formulating a series of short-term goals that will lead to the life goals, and knowing one's financial base. This latter involves listing assets and liabilities as well as creating a monthly budget. Once a budget has been created, financial goals for one year are set and a plan founded on a budget is tested. After one year, the plan is revised and fit into short-term life goals. An evaluation of the plan takes place annually to decide on its continued applicability.

WHO NEEDS FINANCIAL PLANNING?

Financial planning is essential to anyone who wants to achieve life goals that involve money. There is no period during a lifetime when financial plans should not be developed and followed. The use of money for a Christian is a matter of stewardship because the use of money and giving are intimately connected. A financial plan becomes the method for being a good steward.

A financial plan is critical for families because of the pressures on financial resources. Affluent families may not think a plan is essential because their cash flow is high and they can meet monthly obligations rather easily. However, affluence based on high cash flow can be terminated almost instantly. High incomes do not equal assets unless a person or family has decided to build up assets by diverting some of the cash into savings or investments each month.

A financial plan is equally important to single persons and to retired individuals. These types of persons do not have backup sources of finance and must depend upon themselves to meet most emergencies. Without a good financial plan that forces them to save and invest, they may court financial disaster.

WHEN A PLAN NEEDS REVISION

A financial plan needs to be revised when it becomes restrictive and unproductive or when a life goal is changed. The need to change a financial plan most often occurs when a significant event happens in an individual's or a family's life. For example, when an individual is terminated from a job and must take another one that has less pay and fewer benefits, it is time to create a new financial plan. When a single person marries or a married person becomes single it is necessary to create a new financial plan. When a person retires or moves to another geographic area or a child is born or a child leaves home, new financial plans should be developed.

It is time to revise a plan when a change occurs in a person's or a family's finances. For instance, when a family goes from two to one worker the financial plan must be adjusted. A budget cannot be out of joint for even a short time without serious financial consequences to the life pattern of the individual or the family. Therefore, the budget must be changed. This change signals a need to revise the financial plan.

SUMMARY

Financial planning is an important part of the stewardship activities of individuals and of churches. The role of the pastor in financial planning is to inform people about the need to do it and to give them some basic how-tos. Developing a program for the church is the focus of the next discussion.

Chapter 6

A CHURCH PROGRAM
IN FINANCIAL PLANNING

"We ought to include financial planning as part of our stewardship program."

"Not on your life! People are too sensitive about their money to talk about it at church."

"Why? They have to look at their finances pretty carefully every time they make a pledge."

"I'm not certain about that. If they looked at their finances all that carefully and thought about stewardship, most of them would give a lot more than they do to the church."

"Maybe. I'll bet that a part of their reluctance to talk about their money is probably due to their feeling that they don't have enough to raise their pledge. Many of them probably feel overcommitted already. Therefore, it seems to me that a church wanting to increase its pledges will help people plan their finances."

"You sound like a lawyer, but logic doesn't always win out when money is concerned. I think people will resist any church sponsored financial planning program because they don't feel church leaders know that much about financial planning."

"But if we had some experts in financial planning

conduct a series of workshops, wouldn't that make a difference? I think it's a shame for a church like ours not even to try to have a program for financial planning."

Many pastors have found themselves wondering whether or not their church should sponsor a program for financial planning. They should not be hesitant. This kind of program makes sense for the church to sponsor if for no other reason than its own self-interest. The self-interest argument is that financial planning will increase the probability that people will feel they can increase their contributions to the church and its programs.

A more powerful argument, however, is grounded in Christian stewardship. A good stewardship program in a church will include financial planning because this type of planning assists church members to be better stewards of their resources. It is reasonable to expect, for example, that a stewardship program that admonishes people to give 5 or 10 percent of their income to the church will provide the guidelines needed to help those members develop a financial plan that makes those percentages become realities instead of possibilities.

Every church, of course, will not feel that it is convenient or appropriate to sponsor a program on financial planning. These congregations will be swayed by the objections of a few individuals to justify their decision not to sponsor such programs. For example, churches in which several influential members have retained financial consultants and tax lawyers might not want to engage in financial planning programming. Their argument is that the members do not need any more help. This is unfortunate since a Christian attitude of stewardship toward the use of money may be quite different from the concepts proposed by secular tax consultants and financial advisers. Besides, those members who do not have tax consultants and tax lawyers to assist them would find such programs helpful. Indeed, it would be the rare congregation that could not benefit from a program on financial planning.

WHO SHOULD BE THE LEADER?

In many churches the pastor may be qualified to lead this program if he or she has had experience or training in budgeting and financial planning. Unfortunately, many pastors have neither. Therefore, it is best to search for leaders who are not pastors.

Pastors with financial planning experience and who insist that they are qualified sometimes do lead financial planning workshops and seminars. A few of them are effective in their own churches. However, it is recommended that most pastors not be leaders in such programs because of the nature of their other contacts with members. Leading a financial planning workshop gives a completely different image of the pastor to members than does leading worship or Christian education and leadership training seminars. Also, when a pastor leads a financial planning course in the church, this may be a turnoff for some members.

On the other hand, who else in the congregation ought to be able to bring as much Christian stewardship insight to finances as the pastor? Pastors have a role, especially in stewardship education, that impinges on financial planning, but this role is not leading financial planning workshops or courses in their church. Their primary role is more critical: They must emphasize the need for financial planning as an ingredient in the stewardship program of the church.

Assume for the moment that the pastor, as a leader in the stewardship program of the church, convinces the governing body of the congregation to sponsor a financial planning program. Where can the church turn for the kind of leadership it can feel will be helpful from a Christian stewardship perspective? There are multiple possibilities.

Urban communities have church people who are financial planning experts, some of whom advertise and some who do not. A church might want to turn to these people for leadership. The church, in making its contact with such an individual, will need to clarify the nature of its program and the emphasis it desires the program to have. The leader should not be allowed a totally free hand in setting it up.

An alternative would be to approach the Conference or Synod office for leadership suggestions. While there may not be such a leader on the regional staff, these staff members would know of experts willing to help churches design these types of programs.

Leaders for financial planning programs may be recruited from the business faculty of a local college or university. One or more professors may have a workshop or seminar design they can adapt for use in a church. Often, they conduct these programs for a fee, which can be met by charging participants a small tuition. A church wishing to sponsor such a program without cost to the participants can include it in the educational budget.

National denominational stewardship persons sometimes lead financial planning workshops that are designed to train leaders who, in turn, will conduct seminars in local churches. Training workshops conducted by denominational leaders are usually limited in scope and local church members are not encouraged to attend. These workshops are designed for, and sponsored by, regional denominational persons.

Denominational leaders, however, may also conduct workshops for local church members. These may be offered in conjunction with a stewardship campaign or as part of a stewardship education emphasis. The denominational leader may be from the regional or national offices.

Recruiting appropriate leadership is not an issue for a pastor who wants to create a program in financial planning in his or her church. More important is making the decision that such a program will be helpful to church members. The pastor's primary role, as stated earlier, is to assist the church in deciding to pursue a financial planning program. This decision is the first step in establishing the program.

GENERAL DESIGN OF THE PROGRAM

There are six major components of a course or workshop on financial planning. These include an explanation and a definition of the concept of financial planning; the procedures for creating and following a budget; various techniques that will assist one in managing money (checking accounts, electronic banking, computerized checkbooks, and so on); investing (mutual funds, creating a portfolio, using a broker, real estate, savings accounts, money market accounts, certificates of deposits); insurance (liability, accident, property, personal, catastrophe, endowment); and taxes. These may be dealt with in a one-day seminar or in a course with several sessions, usually one evening each week for a month.

A brief course in financial planning will include sessions on each of the various aspects of financial planning. Normally the course is limited to four sessions with insurance and taxes being combined with other items. In some situations, these two are treated separately and advertised as self-contained seminars without mention of their association with financial planning.

A one-day seminar may allot an hour for each of the six major topics. The advantage of this tactic is to provide an overview of the total financial planning process for those who attend. There is not time to get into detail or to have much opportunity to practice any of the techniques that are presented. A disadvantage is that a one-day seminar that presents this much information tends to expose most people to more than they can comprehend and put into operation.

Another version of a financial planning workshop focuses on definitions and the procedures for creating a household or personal budget. The advantage of this approach is that only one topic is dealt with. The primary focus of the presentation is on explaining guidelines that may be followed in creating a budget. There is also time for participants to practice setting up their own personal budget. The course leader is available during the day as a personal consultant.

A multi-session course will include in each meeting guidelines and illustrations that make each part of the financial planning process understandable. In most sessions, time is provided so that participants may practice financial planning using their own situation. In an effective course, an individual will have completed a preliminary financial plan by the time the course is finished.

A complete course however is rarely offered. Workshops conducted by most nonchurch leaders are one day or a few hours in duration. Their aim is to acquaint people with the basic elements of budget building and the rudiments of financial planning. More advanced seminars and workshops may be advertised as continuations of initial workshops, but usually additional sessions are for specific aspects of financial planning such as investing, insurance, and taxes. This format is typical of professors, people who advertise themselves as financial planners, denominational leaders, and representatives of banks or brokerage houses.

Most leaders of financial planning workshops, seminars, and courses have designed and make available (usually for a fee) materials to guide anyone interested in actually engaging in financial planning. Such materials are simple and easy to follow but are limited in scope. They may be forms for listing assets and liabilities, formats for creating budgets, and reprints of articles on insurance, budget-building, and investing. These materials tend to have limited value for persons who have not been participants in the leader's workshop. The materials are most helpful to the person who is comparing various techniques of different leaders in financial planning rather than to the individual who wants to learn how to plan.

Another type of program is the self-study course, which may come as a series of audio or video cassettes. These are normally audio or video prints of workshop presentations the leaders have had taped. The leaders have edited the presentations and make them available commercially. These tapes present an alternative to a church that has one or more persons who are experts in one or more of the topics to be discussed. A church class or an adult education course may utilize these tapes, having the experts available to help people during a practice session.

Videotapes, especially, are helpful to churches because churches need not spend a great deal of money to engage a leader to conduct a seminar. Videotapes have proven so helpful to participants that some leaders suggest to them that they purchase them as re-enforcements to what they have learned. In addition to re-enforcement, the tapes provide revenue for workshop leaders. Videotaped courses may be available from the denomination's stewardship office.

SPECIFIC NEEDS ADDRESSED

A difficulty of many financial planning programs is their disregard for the differences in life situations of participants. Income and liabilities may vary widely among participants. Disparities in income tend to be especially intimidating to some participants. Also, different age groups exhibit specific and unusual differences in incomes and liabilities. Investing and the use of money management techniques are directed at different goals by individuals and families of different ages. These variations are either overlooked or assumed not to be critical by most financial planning persons.

A financial planning program in the church cannot make that assumption. An effective, church-sponsored financial planning program must be designed to be sensitive to the variety of backgrounds and life situations of the participants. Of course, it is impractical to try to design a program with a separate course for each age group and life situation category represented in the church. However, it is possible, and necessary, to define some categories and direct a program toward each.

The most effective method of accomplishing customized training for a diverse group is to divide each session into two parts. The first part of the session presents general information needed for one aspect of financial planning. For instance, the first part of the budgeting session would provide data and guidelines important to everyone attempting to create a budget. The second part of the session is devoted to practicing budget-building. It is this part in which customizing can occur. Persons with similar needs are grouped together during this time period. As they work in small groups or by themselves, participants can relate to others who have similar needs and opportunities.

For example, participants in a church sponsored program who are between twenty and thirty years of age and who are single may attend the same course as individuals who are retired. Part one of the session is the same for all participants since it deals with theory and general applications. This part of the presentation might delineate general guidelines one follows to create a budget. During part two of the session, however, in which people are asked to actually design a budget, the younger people are separated from the older folks because their life situations are quite different. Examples and long-term goals used in each group are significantly divergent even though both groups are setting up personal budgets. This process of dividing the group during practice customizes a course.

The technique of general presentation followed by group work can be used for each aspect of financial planning including investing, money management, taxes, and insurance. In order to be fully customized, the program ought to give participants the option of being in one of two or three different groups during practice. In unusual situations, such as when most of the participants have limited incomes, the program should be further customized by emphasizing strategies of budgeting, investing, and money management that are realistically within their reach.

The most effective church sponsored financial planning seminar or course will be built around the needs and circumstances of the potential participants. This requires prior planning and work by the pastor and the leader.

The leader will do whatever customizing of the course is possible or necessary. He or she will decide the types of guidelines and illustrations that are needed as well as how many groups will be used during the practice session. The leader must be willing to give as much planning time as is needed to make the course effective for participants.

A pastor's role, at this point, is to help the course leaders design a program that is appropriate and useful for the church members. This means the pastor must study the materials the leaders will use and have a knowledge of the various life situations of church members. The pastor can be very helpful by assisting the leader to understand the possible participants in terms of life patterns and situations. The pastor may rely on suggestions from potential participants in advising leaders on the direction the course should take.

A church may decide to offer a series of courses for different age groups rather than attempt to customize parts of a single course. The multi-course approach is preferable in certain larger churches because it allows a leader to focus on a particular group throughout the entire course. This gives the leader more time to work with all of the participants rather than trying to be in each of the smaller (and different) work groups during every session of a multi-faceted course.

Another option is for a church to work with a college, university, or another congregation in sponsoring one or more segments of a financial planning course. In this approach, an entire course is developed and offered but with different leaders and at various meeting places. The course may take an entire year to complete, but each segment is offered at least three times during that period.

This is customizing because the segment on budgeting, for example, is designed for a different group each time it is offered. A church can sponsor financial planning in conjunction with other organizations. Thus, the church will choose that segment that may be most beneficial to its own members, such as budgeting, or it may choose to provide the beginning session, which introduces the need and concept of financial planning. In addition, the church can decide when to offer the segment. This will make the program fit into its schedule and provide more convenience for members wishing to participate in it. In any case, participants are encouraged to attend the other course meetings in order to acquire the information offered by the entire course.

FREQUENCY OF PROGRAM OFFERINGS

The size and mobility of a congregation are to be considered when decisions are made about the frequency with which a financial planning program is offered. A large congregation of more than 1,500 members may offer a general course and two specialized segments once every two years. A church with 500 to 1,500 members may offer a general course every other year. A congregation with fewer than 500 members in a stable community may offer a general course every four years.

A financial planning course ought to be offered when unusual economic conditions strike a community. For instance, when a new industry begins or an old one leaves the economics of a community are drastically changed and people need some assistance in planning for the new situation. At such times, it is important that the church help people realistically adjust to their changed financial situations. A course in financial planning at this juncture is appropriate as a part of the church's ministry.

A CHURCH PROGRAM IN FINANCIAL PLANNING

A congregation in a community that experiences rapid growth of a particular age group, for example, retired persons or young married couples, would do well to offer financial planning courses aimed at the needs of these groups. The course for people retired and moving into a new setting would help acquaint them with their new economic surroundings, any changes in living costs they could expect in contrast to those of their last place of residence, the kind and impact of local property and other taxes, and investment possibilities. A course for young married couples would emphasize money management so they could maximize their income, how to deal effectively with living costs that rise as a family matures, and investments in which long-term growth is the goal. The church, by addressing new residents through a financial planning program, would be engaged in a significant outreach ministry.

A congregation, in spite of its desire to include financial planning in its program offerings, must be sensitive to the needs of its members and its community. Other churches or agencies may be offering such a program as well. The availability of the course elsewhere may affect the frequency with which a church offers a course in financial planning. On the other hand, just because a course has been offered once or is offered by another agency does not make it unnecessary to sponsor it again. A strategy for programming will include such a course at least every three years in most churches' adult education offerings.

EVALUATING THE PROGRAM

This program, like all others in the church, will be evaluated with regard to leadership, materials, direction, appropriateness, and content. The evaluation should be done by securing feedback from participants and collecting data from observers. The leader's feelings, too, will be an important source of information about the effectiveness of the course. The evaluation of this program should be done with the same frequency as that used for other church programs. It should not be singled out for special attention just because it focuses on money.

Evaluation may be conducted by an outside agency or by the administrative council of the congregation. It will be important to conduct this evaluation thoroughly if the program is sponsored as a part of the education budget of the church. Its effectiveness will need to be weighed against other important adult education courses.

SUMMARY

A financial planning program is an important addition to the stewardship program in every church. It teaches people about budgeting, money management, savings, and investing. It needs to be customized because age and life situations influence both the amount of money and the kinds of liabilities of an individual or of a family. This program ought to be offered at least every three years but may be given more frequently depending upon the growth, economic situation, and size of a church and its community. It must be evaluated with the same tenacity and thoroughness that other church programs are.

$

PART 3
Wills

"Wills are for old people. I don't want to think about them now."

"You'd better think about them. Wills are a necessary part of everyone's financial planning."

"Why?"

"Because only through a will can a person designate to whom and for what money and tangible assets will go at death. If you don't have a will, much of your money will be lost to lawyers and tied up in court."

In spite of many cautions like this, only about a third of the adults in this nation have made wills. This has resulted in hardships and great loss of assets because of the way in which states have written their laws for dividing up estates for which there are no wills. Every state government has a procedure for freezing bank accounts, sealing safe deposit boxes, and making it impossible to use any existing assets until the government has made a determination of the possible living beneficiaries, the veracity of their identity and relationship to the deceased, and paid the outstanding liabilities of the deceased. These procedures require lawyers, who use up a portion of the estate. In brief, the manner in which the state makes these distributions does not often reflect the desires of the deceased.

In light of this reality, a responsible pastor must encourage church members to make wills. The reasons for this admonition are to ensure that the desires of the deceased are reflected in the way assets are divided, to facilitate closing of the estate and allowing recipients to use money and other assets, and to continue a giving life pattern. This latter issue, continuing a giving life pattern, is discussed in detail in my earlier book, *The Tithe: Challenge or Legalism?* (Abingdon Press, 1984).

A pastor needs to understand what a will is and does. A will is a legal document in which an individual outlines the way in which property and other assets are to be divided among survivors following his or her death. Most wills focus solely on tangible assets such as money, real estate, and other possessions. A will, however, may include other directives such as specific instructions about disposing of the body and organ donations.

A will is legally binding although it may be contested if a relative feels that undue influence was exercised by someone so that the will does not reflect the perceived wishes of the deceased. This is a relatively common occurrence. Usually, a court must determine the validity of the claims of the accuser. In the absence of a will, such legal contests have sometimes used all of the estate so that the winner and the loser in the court fight receive identical settlements—nothing.

A will is an extension of the influence of an individual beyond death. In this form, the will can be used to encourage Christian living and giving patterns among the survivors. For instance, donating organs for use by another person is one form of Christian witness and leaving money to a specific mission-oriented organization is another.

The basics of will making, an important act in an individual's or a family's life, is the subject of the next chapter. As emphasized below, a will is for everyone, although its contents must be altered according to changing life ideas and patterns.

Chapter 7

BASICS OF WILL MAKING

Writing an uncomplicated will is a relatively simple and swift task. Individuals go to a lawyer, who asks them for information such as the names of persons who are to be named as beneficiaries, the extent of the estate, and their desires about the distribution of the assets. The lawyer then writes the will, which is signed by the person for whom the will was written. As soon as the individual signs, another person, a legally disinterested party usually chosen by the lawyer, witnesses it.

The entire process of will making may take an hour's time for an individual or family, including some typing time by the lawyer's secretary, about half an hour of composition and checking by the lawyer, and about five minutes for a witness. The hour, however, may be spread over two to three weeks because of the need for the lawyer to make certain the will contains the exact wishes of the individual making the will. The process is routine for law offices that deal with wills.

Creating a complicated will can be time consuming. Complications are caused when relatively large amounts of money are involved, the number and types of nonmonetary possessions to be given away are diverse, and there are a number of possible claimants for parts of an estate such as real estate or stock portfolios. These complications add time and effort on the part of the lawyer and the person or persons for whom the will is written. Care must be taken to ensure that the exact wishes of the person are incorporated into the will.

An additional complication exists for some persons. Wills for estates that contain several pieces of property and money in stocks or bonds must consider the consequences of taxes on the assets by federal and state governments. These wills may take several months to put together and involve tax lawyers, because trusts may need to be created in order for the distribution of assets to be most beneficial to the survivors.

A will, because it is not concerned solely with money, can be written to identify people who should care for minor children, to specify that organs be donated, to indicate the kind of body disposition one desires, such as cremation or burial in another state, or other items of importance to an individual. As a legally binding document, a will imposes one's wishes upon survivors, at least in those things the individual feels most strongly about, following death.

Some people believe that creating a will is as easy as going to a stationery store and purchasing a form, completing it, having it witnessed, and putting it in a safe deposit box. While this is better than having no will, most people need a customized will rather than a standard will. The reasons for demanding that a will be customized will become clearer as we consider what ought to be included in a will.

WHEN TO WRITE THE WILL

A will can be written at any point in life. It is a personal document that becomes a safety net for one's survivors. The will specifies how assets are to be used and who gets what from one's estate. The discipline needed to write a will helps the person doing the writing to think about his or her life goals and what he or she wants to accomplish with any remaining assets after death. For the survivors, knowing that a will has been written assures them that most likely they will not spend a lot of money and time on attorney's fees and in court. When there is no will, courts have to decide how to divide up the personal assets of a deceased individual.

A person's first will should be written when he or she becomes an adult. Adulthood is legally defined as beginning between eighteen and twenty-one years of age. Marriage without the need of parental consent, joining the armed services, and being eligible for certain kinds of credit are events predicated on one's age being between these limits. Age limits that signal the beginning of adulthood are written in state laws and vary from state to state.

Unfortunately, most people do not write a will early in life because they believe they do not have enough money or possessions to need one. This is not true. All of us have one or two possessions that we consider valuable. Think carefully about personal possessions. How would most people dispose of their personal possessions such as auto, a wardrobe, or jewelry in the event they died? The majority of people in this nation have not thought about these items as possessions that need to be given away or sold upon their deaths. But possessions must be disposed of once death occurs, which is the reason for writing a will.

Dying may not be a pleasant thought, but it is inevitable, and preparing for it by writing a will is practical. Because death can occur at any age, people need to have their wishes about the use of their possessions put into a legally binding form; that is, a will. After all, people have feelings about who they want to use or have their possessions when death does occur. Being aware of these feelings makes creating a will a worthy consideration at any age.

Whenever the circumstances of an individual or family change, it is also a good time to write (or rewrite) a will. For example, getting married is one of those times. After marriage, there will be a change in the beneficiary or manner in which the sequence of beneficiaries is determined. It is probable, as well, that income and assets will change markedly. These changes need to be reflected in a will.

The birth of a child should result in a new will. The budding family will need to make certain that the parental possessions are bequeathed for the benefit of the child or children in the event of death of either or both parents. The new lives added to the family need protection and care until they can assume management of their personal affairs. The parents, through their will, need to make certain that children have enough sustenance as well as supervision until they come of age.

When parents of minor children—usually those under age twenty-one—create a will, they must identify people who will provide oversight for those children until they become adults. This means the parents must decide upon an individual or family who can be charged with raising the children to adulthood in case of the untimely death of both parents. This designation of foster parents must be done carefully because the parents want the children to be raised with a particular life pattern and values. Consequently, the names of possible foster parents in a will may need to be changed several times before the children reach adulthood.

Changing the designation of foster parents in a will may be necessary because of changing relationships between the parents and the potential parents, the physical or psychological health of children or possible foster parents or both, or the death of the designated foster parents. Parents may want to designate an older child as the protector and foster parent of minor children. Thus, parents of minor children must be aware of changes in their own feelings as well as the age of their children. What is appropriate at one age in a child's life may not be appropriate in another. The will should reflect current reality as much as possible.

A divorce is another opportune time for writing a will. A new life situation has been created by the divorce and the will must reflect the changed circumstances of the family. This is particularly important if children are involved. Taking care of them until they reach adulthood or making certain they are included in the inheritance must be considered in a new will. In addition, the list of beneficiaries in a will changes after a divorce. For this reason if for no other, a will should either be written or changed at this time.

A change of job, especially if income is greatly increased, and the purchase of property are other times when it becomes advantageous to write a will. These changes increase the value of one's assets; thus, how they are to be dispersed in the event of death needs careful attention. Any time an estate increases in value, the potential for several persons wanting a piece of it increases. A will is written to protect those persons to whom an individual wants to give the bulk of the estate.

In short, an individual who is married, who has children, who has property, who is employed, or who wants to influence the way in which his or her possessions are used after death should write a will. It needs to be written now, not tomorrow or the next day. A will is a document, not a mental exercise that is only spoken. It demands that a person or a family set down in writing their desires about the way their possessions should be distributed after their deaths. Good intentions about writing a will are not enough. It has to be written before it becomes binding upon anyone.

WHO SHOULD WRITE THE WILL?

Stories about persons who, on their death beds, dictate a will to a nurse or who write their will on a scrap of paper are heard often but are rarely based on fact. The physical condition of the individual and the demands of care by those in attendance make such a scenario quite difficult.

Seldom do people in such circumstances have enough energy and presence of mind to write a will that can be defended in court.

It is a fact that individuals have written wills on whatever material has been available prior to death. These last-minute wills can be overturned or at least contested when a previous will naming other beneficiaries is discovered. The primary problems with writing a last-minute will are that it needs to be witnessed by a legally disinterested party and it must include the whole estate. These requirements, particularly the legally disinterested party, may negate or put into question a perfectly legal will when the person witnessing it is in fact not disinterested, but included as a beneficiary.

An individual who wants to use a standardized form can do so with few legal complications if he or she knows the laws of the state in which the will becomes binding. Learning about these laws can mean visits to the local library or having conversations with a lawyer. (Because most lawyers charge for giving advice it would be wiser to pay him or her to write the will rather than asking questions so one can do it alone.) Also, finding a disinterested witness, legally speaking, is a hurdle for those using a standardized form.

It is usually expedient for a person desiring to create a will to find a good lawyer (based on recommendations of friends) who deals with wills, than to try to write it alone. A lawyer knows the legal requirements of the state, has experience with wills, and can point out the positive and negative legal ramifications of one's wishes. The cost of a lawyer's time to write a will is more than repaid by the limited need for lawyers when the will is put into effect by death.

Using a lawyer to create a will is not complicated. A person makes an appointment to discuss creating a will with a lawyer who has been recommended or whom he or she has done research on (call the state bar association to ask about his or her record and qualifications) or both. In the first meeting, the person describes what he or she thinks should be put into the will. The lawyer may ask for a list of persons to be included as beneficiaries and a written description of how property should be distributed. The lawyer, after examining the list and the description, asks questions for clarification and, when satisfied, asks the person to return in a week or two.

Between these meetings, the lawyer drafts the will. The individual receives a call to come to the lawyer's office to review the draft with the lawyer and to finalize the contents of the will. The person should plan to spend enough time at this second meeting to make certain what is said is understood and that the lawyer incorporates the person's true wishes into the document.

It takes about another week following this conversation for the lawyer to put the will into final form. After the person receives the lawyer's call to come to sign the will, he or she goes to the office and reads it through with the lawyer again to make certain one last time that it includes everything it must. If something the person thinks is important has been excluded, he or she asks that the will be redrafted. Redrafting a will at this point may save much time later on. After the person has read it and said that it is acceptable, the lawyer calls in a witness. The individual is asked to sign the will and the witness then signs it. The lawyer retains a copy, oftentimes the original (depending upon state law), in his or her files and gives the person the original or one or two copies. In the future, a person may ask for another copy in case his or her copy is lost.

This procedure of about an hour makes a great difference to survivors upon one's death. The estate, regardless of its size, can be divided according to the provisions of the will by an executor, the person named in the will to carry out its provisions. This person or organization, because he, she, or it is pivotal in decisions regarding the will, must be chosen carefully.

CHOOSING AND CHANGING
EXECUTORS

An executor may be an individual, an institution such as the estate department of a bank, or a lawyer. The executor is charged, by law, to carry out the various instructions of the will. These instructions usually include paying off the obligations of the deceased prior to determining the net value of the estate, providing for taxes and other necessities related to state and federal laws, verifying the identity of the persons named in the will, and dividing up the estate. The duties are not complex, but they do take time. The executor works closely with a lawyer and a bank in handling the details of the will. The key traits of an executor are honesty and responsibility.

Choosing an executor is very important because of the duties he or she assumes. It is advisable to weigh suggestions about an executor from the lawyer who writes the will. This lawyer, because of previous experience, knows the abilities of various organizations to be executors and the kinds of problems that might arise when a will is read. No will can be expected to be received with good feelings by everyone who is involved in its benefits or obligations.

The trust departments of some banks contain specialists in handling estates. They know the tax laws and can assist survivors with investments and methods for paying the taxes of the estate. These departments are not composed of a lone individual and are expected to be around following the death of the person who wrote the will.

Choosing an individual, such as a trusted family friend, as an executor can pose a risk because no one knows when someone else may die. Thus, the executor of an estate may die before the will must be executed. If this happens, the court must assist the survivors in appointing another executor.

A family lawyer may be a sentimental favorite to be the executor of a will, but lawyers are mortals like everyone else and can die too. If the lawyer is a member of a firm, however, the will can be handled by anyone in the firm.

The choice of an executor is not final until the death of the person who writes the will. Changing an executor is as simple as amending the will. This requires another session with the lawyer, reviewing the will, changing the name of the executor, signing the will, and having it witnessed. This process may take minutes for the person writing the will but may save hundreds or thousands of dollars for the survivors.

The important point about executors is to trust these persons or organizations enough to allow them to have control over one's possessions after death. They are going to make judgments that may be costly to the survivors. The writer of a will must be convinced beforehand that the executor to be named has the long-term interests of the will writer in mind.

REVISING A WILL

Any change in life dictates the need to change a will. For example, changing jobs may involve a significant difference in compensation, travel, or number of obligations. The job change may require a family to move from an inexpensive to an expensive place in another part of the nation. Such a move might mean increasing the size of one's mortgage. Making certain the total cost of a mortgage is covered without requiring the survivors to assume a large debt is one aspect of a will. The job change, in this situation, demands changes in the will.

A couple who decide to take a tour in another country will need to examine the provisions of their wills. They may have to make significant changes in them because of small children. They need to make certain the children are cared for until they reach adulthood. This means choosing appropriate foster parents.

Every time a family increases by adding a member or decreases by losing a member, the wills of the parents need revision. Anytime a marriage occurs or breaks up, an individual's will must reflect this change.

Revising a will is done in the same sequence and takes the same amount of time as writing a new will. In effect, this is what happens: The new will retains parts of the old but adds appropriate items to reflect changes in the life pattern of the person writing the will.

The cost of writing a will or revising it runs from $200 to $500. This seems costly to many persons but is a small price for assuring an orderly distribution of one's possessions and the carrying out of one's wishes with regard to survivors.

CHRISTIAN GIVING THROUGH A WILL

A will is designed to distribute one's assets to various survivors. These survivors, for a Christian, ought to include churches or church related organizations. A Christian whose life has been predicated on giving can continue this pattern by remembering various organizations and institutions through the will. Death is final for the physical body but through a will one's spirit and intent in life can be extended.

It is not necessary to own a large estate in order to give. Designating some money for a church's scholarship program can increase the principle enough to allow another young person to attend college. This does not require a great deal of money, since even a modest gift can be added to existing monies.

Setting aside a piece of real estate or a valuable personal possession so that a church or church related agency can sell it or use it is another alternative. This type of gift may be more useful in the long term than money. For example, a small tract of land could become the site for a retreat center, a gardening plot, or an income producing parcel. These uses might expand the mission and ministry of a church much more than an equivalent gift of money.

The person who creates a will must be reminded by the pastor that it can contain provisions for giving to the church. In this way, the person's lifetime of giving may continue for some years following his or her death.

SUMMARY

A will is a necessity for people who are interested in financial planning. The will can specify how the assets of an estate (of any size) should be distributed. A will can be written at any point in life and needs to be revised when there is a significant change in one's life pattern. An important consideration in writing a will is naming an executor, the person or organization responsible for following the precepts and directives of the will. A will can be changed by writing a new one that supersedes the existing one. Wills can be revised up to the time of death. A giving life pattern should be continued through a will. This idea is discussed in more detail in *The Tithe: Challenge or Legalism,* chapter 6.

Chapter 8

WILLS AT DIFFERENT AGES

Life is constantly changing and with the changes come new challenges, opportunities, and difficulties. Many of life's changes are predictable because they usually overtake persons of the same age. These predictable changes are those over which one has some control such as getting married, deciding to have children, taking and changing jobs, accumulating assets, and the like. Enough statistical evidence exists to point out to people the kinds of events that are most probable when they reach young adulthood, middle age, and older ages.

An individual can prepare, at least a bit, for the predictable events in life. Getting married can be planned for as can the birth of a child. Financial planning can assist in accumulating assets for use if illness strikes or for use in older ages. The predictable events are incorporated into most people's life plans.

There are many other events that cannot be predicted and over which one has no control. These include natural disasters, shifts in the economy that may result in the loss of jobs, or death. The sighting of a tornado may be broadcast, but its path and ultimate destructiveness cannot be forecast. An earthquake can be forecast, but the specific moment or place it will be most severe cannot be pinpointed. Much in life is out of any one person's control. The realization of this fact causes some people to assume a fatalistic approach to life. They believe that to prepare signals a lack of faith in God's design.

A productive life is not fatalistic and cannot dwell upon those things over which one has no control. A person with faith must focus upon those parts of life that can be influenced by his or her direct action. For such persons, a will is one way to maintain their influence over what they possess in life when death intervenes.

The fact of change provides an outline for discussing the need to update a will based upon the kinds of responsibilities and opportunities differing ages bring. The contents of a will must be examined for relevance and comprehensiveness at various stages of life. Data collected through the years have shown that income, financial obligations, and family related responsibilities change as one ages. These statistics can be useful in predicting how an individual should write a will. Examples of two different life situations illustrate a general approach to writing a will at various ages in life.

A single person who wrote a will at the age of twenty-five may be unencumbered by family needs through the age of forty. She has a good job, has a townhouse, owns an auto, has several investments, and can be considered successful in her line of work. Suddenly, not long after her forty-first birthday, she discovers that her parents are becoming dependent upon her. This dependency is related to gifts of money she makes to them, advice she offers in the area of finances or other life situations, her care for the family home by providing help on maintenance and upkeep, her assistance in their planning for the future, and her assistance in providing for their health care needs. This single woman upon discovering their dependency may want to alleviate it, but until that becomes a feasible option she must make changes in her will in order to continue the care of her parents in case something happens to her.

A different situation arises between a young couple who marry. They write wills to reflect their new status in life. Within six years they have three children. As soon as the first child is born, they write wills that direct the family's resources to the surviving spouse, or to foster parents in case both parents die, in order to help the parent or foster parents raise the children to adulthood. When the children are adults, the couple revise their wills to reflect their own increased assets and their changed responsibilities with regard to their children. When the couple retire they need to consider how their remaining assets will be disposed of when they die. Once these decisions have been made, they revise their wills again.

These two situations illustrate the kinds of events that might cause people to write and revise wills. Note in the second example that each partner in marriage writes a will. A will is an individual's document, not a group document, though it influences others by its provisions. It is important to understand that each phase of life presents a new scenario for creating a will.

While there is no "average life situation," it is possible to deal with will making by identifying the needs usually associated with the various life stages. The "age stage" outline can be useful for pastors when they counsel individuals who are interested in creating or revising a will.

THE YOUNG ADULT

The young adult has been defined as being within the approximate ages of twenty and thirty-five years. These young people are beginning adulthood and, as a result, engage in a variety of "starts" during these years. (See also *Ministry with Young Couples,* by Douglas W. Johnson, wherein young adults are divided into three age groups based on the kinds of decisions and responsibilities they have as they move from twenty through thirty-five years.) The various kinds of starts tend to include getting their first full-time jobs and beginning careers, finding mates and getting married or choosing not to be married, and making decisions about having children (which may affect the marital status of those who earlier made a decision not to marry).

In addition to, or as a consequence of, these starts, young adults begin accummulating assets and possessions. They may purchase an automobile when they are in their early twenties and upgrade it as they continue through their young adult years. They will acquire a wardrobe and, perhaps, some jewelry. They may make a decision about donating their organs at death. Each of these decisions, acquisitions, and accumulations results in a specific asset or desire that should be included in a will.

Unless the young adult resides at the parents' home, he or she must find a place to live. He or she may have accumulated, by the late twenties, enough money to begin purchasing a house, condominium, a town house, or other living facility. If a purchase is made, the young person begins to generate equity (a particular type of accumulation, defined in chapter 5). A person does not have to marry before buying a house; however, marrying is when many young adults buy houses. It is then that they begin to accumulate assets at an increasing rate.

The decision to marry is life changing. The marriage ceremony is a visible point of departure from one type of life to another. Although single persons accumulate assets and responsibilities, such accumulations assume new meaning when applied to a married couple. Household appliances, furniture, and accessories such as paintings are likely to be upgraded when a person marries. Instead of one automobile, the family may need two. Rather than shunning the purchase of jewelry, a family may feel the need to buy several pieces just to let others know that the couple are doing well.

The third "start" at which the emphasis on accumulation of possessions is changed again, is when a child or children join the family. The child may be added by birth or adoption—it makes no difference. The family's assets and obligations begin to take on much greater magnitude than either parent dreamed was possible when they were contemplating marrying. Not only do they have themselves to purchase furniture and clothes for, but the child or children must also have additional furniture and clothing. These other purchases become additional assets.

Young adults, quite apart from their choices to marry and have children, accumulate assets on their own volition. They may belong to stock buying clubs, join a stock option plan at work, or live by a rigorous budget, which allows them to save money regularly. When any or all of these habits are followed, their monetary assets will increase at a relatively rapid rate.

The young adult who writes a will has several items to consider. Any asset, including money, furniture, house, automobile, or hobby (such as stamp collecting), must be disposed of. These items can be bequeathed to other family members if the individual is single, given to a church or organization to sell and use the proceeds, divided among several friends, or distributed in any other way the person so desires. The point young adults need to comprehend is that if they do not disperse these items through a will, the courts will inventory the estate, sell the items, and divide the money among a legitimate group of survivors.

The will of a single young adult, although it may be complicated, is not as extensive as the one written by a married young adult. The married young adult must decide whether everything goes to his or her surviving spouse or to others or both. Usually there is a split in the will so that the spouse as well as the parents of the deceased are beneficiaries.

The young adult's will when minor children are involved must name beneficiaries as well as protectors and foster parents for the minor children. Because a will is written with the knowledge that survivors named in the will may precede the will writer in death, alternatives must be included in the will. The alternative beneficiary part of the will, however, should be in the will no matter if the young adult is single, married, or married and with minor children.

A young adult discussing the contents of a will with a lawyer should not overlook possible insurance money. In some circumstances, the insurance carried by companies for employees can add a considerable amount of money to the estate.

The young adult, in summary, needs to consider possessions, dependents, family, friends, and churches as beneficiaries. The young adult must create a list of alternative beneficiaries in the event the original beneficiaries die. The will ought to be comprehensive enough to include assets of all types, and it should be revised at each turning point in the young adult's life.

MIDDLE-AGED ADULTS

The middle-aged adult seems to have more people depending upon him or her than does any comparable age group. Among these dependents are aged parents, spouse or close friends, children, and relatives. Each claimant upon the time and energy of the middle-aged adult feels his or her demands are legitimate and more pressing than the claims of anyone else.

The reason for such pressures is the unique position of middle age. An individual has successfully made the "starts" associated with young adulthood and, according to demographic statistics, is at the height of earning power. Possessions are more abundant than during younger years as homes, autos, furnishings, and other items have accumulated. The middle-aged adult may think otherwise, but the facts point out that this individual tends to have relative abundance.

The children of a middle-aged adult are no longer very

young. They usually leave the parents' home sometime around the parents' fiftieth birthdays. If the grown children attend college, the parents may have extraordinary obligations that must be met. If the children have started families of their own, the parents may be relieved of the burdens of having to provide all their sustenance. On the other hand, if the children's marriages fail, the children may move back home with the parents.

In addition to children, the middle-aged adult may discover new dependencies from aging parents. The parents will be retired and may be in failing health. The demands of finding care for and monitoring these aging parents is a burden for the middle-aged adult. It is one of several significant changes in this age group's responsibilities.

The middle-aged adult may respond to these pressures and changed responsibilities by trying to escape them. Children may be told that because they have reached a particular age, they must be responsible for their own lives. College is a struggle for such children, if it is achieved at all. The middle-aged adult may ignore pleas for assistance from aged parents and tell them the government has programs that will protect them.

Not many middle-aged adults take these routes, but a relatively large number take an alternative route that creates significant change in their lives—divorce. This has become a popular way of changing and complicating family life. In many cases, the middle-aged adult who divorces and remarries inherits children. The phrase "mine, yours, or ours" demonstrates the combinations of children that occur in divorced and remarried families.

A will for a middle-aged adult must make sense of the dependencies as well as accurately identify and assess the assets that are part of an estate. This is not a simple task when there is more than a single set of children, when there has been a change of spouse, and when there is a considerable amount of money and some real estate involved. Drawing up the will can be time consuming, but this time can save a significant amount of lawyer fees later on.

The middle-aged adult has to consider the percentage of the estate that should be given to children (mine, yours, ours), the amount of care aged parents may need, and the needs of the surviving spouse, friends, and church. These percentages may require careful calculation if they are to reflect the true desires of the middle-aged adult.

THE OLDER ADULT

Older adults, those persons who have reached at least sixty years of age, should have revised their wills at least twice. The first revision was at marriage and the second was when children were born. Those who have divorced should have changed the will again and those who have remarried should have changed it once more after remarrying. Each change in one's life situation demands a change in the will. The older adult may be retired or nearly retired. Accumulations, such as a house, tend to be paid for, investments have some history, and obligations have lessened as children have gotten their starts. The older adult is faced with the prospect of his or her death. It is time to make certain that one's pattern of living is continued—through the will.

The older adult may decide that children and family members do not need very much of his or her possessions. This decision frees the older adult to channel assets to places and persons where help can mean the difference between mere survival and a better life-style. The opportunity to make this kind of decision about one's assets is not generally available to younger persons because of the pressures of obligations.

An older adult may decide to sell a home and retire in another place. This may change the type of assets to be distributed by the will and may change the will so that the person's body be returned to a home cemetery. These kinds of changes may alter the allocations or percentages of assets going to various parties.

Not unlike persons of other age groups, an older adult does not have a static will because life is constantly changing. Executors may die, grandchildren may be born, children may die, losses of assets may occur, or any number of events may take place before an older adult dies. The will of an older adult is never completed until his or her day of death. It is important for this person, if he or she has not examined the will recently, to review it carefully.

SUMMARY

Wills are for everyone, but the kinds and number of people's possessions and responsibilities vary according to age. A will should reflect the life situation and experience of an individual. While the discussion in this chapter has focused on age categories, it remains critical for everyone to write a will as a part of his or her financial plan. The pastor has a unique opportunity to indicate this need as part of the stewardship education program of the church. It is to this program that we turn next.

$

PART 4
Stewardship Education

"What is stewardship education?"

"That's a good question! It's asked by most pastors sometime during the first few years they are in the ministry. It's relatively easy to answer, too. Stewardship education is teaching Christian people the meaning of sharing and conserving."

"What's so different about stewardship education and living a Christian life?"

"There isn't a difference, except in focus. Stewardship education deals with possessions and environment. The principles of Christian living as taught by Jesus tended to be most concerned with interpersonal and intrapersonal relationships. Once in a while he talked about possessions but mostly in a reproachful manner."

"Then stewardship education is an interpretation of Jesus' message. It really deals with an extension of what he preached about. Is that correct?"

"That's right. Teaching about stewardship is a logical and small jump from Jesus' basic message."

Stewardship, as these pastors are defining it, is based on the implications of Jesus' teachings rather than on Jesus' explicit messages or sayings. Jesus implied that God's world should be protected and that giving a part of one's possessions is expected of a disciple, but these were not central to what he was about. Jesus did not dwell on teaching stewardship.

What Jesus said was that money and possessions can inhibit an individual's relationships with others and can cloud the person's image of God's purpose. Jesus implied that money and possessions are where many people's hearts are. They want to accumulate and display money and possessions. They want so much to get and accumulate that they forget the more important parts of life. Jesus' parables of rich people illustrated his feeling that those who accumulate money and possessions are one-sided people unless they learn to share.

Jesus taught that a life of giving is blessed in God's sight. This makes stewardship's emphasis on sharing one's possessions with others through the church an extension of Jesus' teachings. Unfortunately, stewardship education has not been given this broad an interpretation by many people. They believe stewardship is a concept to be trotted out when pledge time comes around and used to coax money out of church members. Even though this may be how the term is used by some, good stewardship is not a set of gimmicks for fund raising.

It is to offset this narrow meaning of stewardship that this section on stewardship education is included in a book on finance in the church. A significant problem with the term *stewardship* is that it has become so narrow that new ideas about its meaning must be taught. The church and its pastors must broaden their understanding of Christian stewardship before much of what has been discussed in previous chapters can become realities for church members. Two tasks of education are: (1) helping people change their attitudes, and (2) providing the kinds of information that enable people to justify those changes. Therefore, we deal here with the kinds of concepts and techniques churches may find useful in retraining pastors and laity to think in broad stewardship terms. Stewardship education must assist people to incorporate those items discussed in previous chapters into their normal living patterns.

The pastor, because of the pivotal nature of his or her position in church programming, will need to help design the stewardship education program in the church. The following chapters can be used as guides for the designing process.

Chapter 9

TYPES
OF EDUCATION NEEDED

The critical element in any education program is its need to present the same content every year. This is the challenge of any education program although inexperienced teachers and some pastors are uncomfortable with repetition. Repetition is the key to good education. People learn as the same ideas and values are presented in a variety of ways year after year.

Values, the heart of the church's education program, do not change annually, although the manner in which they are expressed evolves over time. For example, the concept of equality among people is a basic Christian value included in Jesus' message. The way in which churches and people have expressed that equality has changed over the centuries and is still evolving.

It is difficult for Christian educators to teach the same concepts year after year because they begin to believe the concepts are "old-fashioned." These educators fail to understand that the concepts are timeless and that it is the techniques for interpreting and helping people understand them that are culture and era bound. The techniques for teaching may be "old-fashioned" even though the basics being communicated continue to be current.

There is an important distinction between the content of teaching (values) and teaching techniques. Techniques include the use of books, pamphlets, and audiovisuals to communicate values. The types of communication needed in stewardship education must be able to transmit the two values of sharing and preserving. While these are critical values to a Christian, they are basic to all human life. In fact, they are taught within families before a child learns to speak. Without sharing there is no family, and without preservation of the environment there are no resources to allow a family to survive.

If the values of sharing and preserving, basic to stewardship, are taught in families, why must the church design an education program to teach them to its members? A detailed example may help answer this question. Families teach their children to speak, to write, and to do arithmetic. This kind of teaching does not eliminate the need for schools. Schools build upon and sometimes correct the teachings a child receives from a family. For example, schools are entrusted with children so that children may learn not only how to speak well, to write correctly, and to figure accurately, but also how to live together with others, how sharing is essential in life, and other basic precepts of a culture.

The church, as it fulfills its educational tasks, imbues people with an interpretation of life that is distinct from the popular cultures. The stewardship emphasis in a church's program moves far beyond the ideas of sharing taught within a family or a play group. A major difference in the content of the teaching of these groups is that the church is concerned with sharing and giving to those who do not live close by and to those who are in no way like the giver. In blunt language, the church's understanding of stewardship is not bound by the natural selfishness of a family or small group. It bursts the bounds of self-centeredness and makes people aware that God's world encompasses all humans. No other institution has this task or performs this function.

TYPES OF EDUCATION NEEDED

Stewardship deals not only with money and personal possessions but also with holdings that people have in common, such as the physical and social environment in which Christians live. When the church teaches stewardship of the environment, it is not limited to popular and easy slogans. It can question the practices of any group or agency. Indeed, the church can speak out against any corporation or government or group or person whose actions or policies desecrate God's creation. The power to do something about preserving and conserving the creation may not rest solely with the church, but its stewardship education program can teach church members to be sensitive to these issues and instill a sense of outrage in them. These factors, sensitivity and outrage, generate within people and groups the power to act in the name of the church.

These broad concepts of stewardship are based on the implications of Jesus' teachings about an individual's responsibility toward neighbors and toward God. A good steward is concerned with possessions in the broadest sense of that concept.

Stewardship education needs to teach the same concepts to every age group each year. Even if the message has been taught for several centuries, it does not take hold without a new interpretation to each new generation and continual reiteration to all living generations. This is the task of stewardship education in every church.

AGE SPECIFIC NEEDS

The three categories of persons in the church, children, youth, and adults, are adequate but not very advantageous for program development purposes. Each includes too many years for effective programming. For instance, the category for children includes babies through sixth graders or eighth graders. This is a wide span of years and represents a great jump in experience. The adult category includes even more years, beginning with eighteen-year-olds and extending through people in their early eighties. Even so, the educational program of most congregations roughly follows these breaks. It is for this reason the three age breaks will be used (though further divided) in this discussion.

1. Children

The church, as it seeks to educate children in stewardship, begins in the nursery years (up to five years) with an emphasis on getting along and sharing. These concepts are difficult for very young children to understand because their life has been, up to this point, totally self-centered. Helping a child learn to give up a toy or to share it with several others is a basic tenet of stewardship education at this time. Learning is by doing, that is, sharing and giving.

During the early elementary years (ages five through nine), children accumulate skills rapidly. They learn to read, write, and compute. These skills can be used in the church's stewardship education program as the children are taught more complex ideas about sharing and giving. They can hone their reading skills by reading simple leaflets that explain stewardship principles. Their interest in heroes can be the starting point for stories about Jesus' sharing and about other persons whose lives revolved around giving, such as Albert Schweitzer.

These early years are when the concept of sharing should be taught in a tangible way. A church can have children of these ages bring clothing, food, or money once a month to share with persons in the community who are less fortunate. When the sharing is thus purposeful and specific, or tangible, children become conscious of the message more than when they hear it only through stories.

In the later elementary years (ages ten through twelve), beginning about fourth grade, stewardship instruction should include helping as well as giving. Active projects, such as work days to assist older folks do chores—cutting grass or sweeping up leaves for example—are useful in pointing out the Christian's intent to care for others. This is the age when activities are as important as discussions and tend to have a longer lasting effect.

It is possible, at these ages, to talk about money and to stress that giving a part of it to others is one part of Christian stewardship. While most children who are ten to twelve years of age do not have a regular income, they may receive an allowance or make money occasionally by raking leaves, shoveling snow, washing windows, or engaging in similar tasks. Because they are working for their money, many of these preteens can equate money with the use of time and energy. When this occurs they can be taught to give to others who may have little opportunity to earn a living.

It is not too early at these ages to start the discussion of budgeting and handling money responsibly. These are aspects of stewardship education that will be developed in more detail as the years pass. However, habits acquired and lessons learned in pre-adolescence shape attitudes and life patterns of later years. It is not wise to exclude budgeting from stewardship education at this level.

The final elementary years (ages thirteen to fourteen) are a time to build upon what has been learned earlier. The stewardship education program should again emphasize sharing, giving, and being responsible for one's assets. Also, by the time young people have reached thirteen years of age they should have been taught about the care and preservation of the environment. This emphasis should complement the more traditional teachings about money and use of time.

Thus, a stewardship education program for children of elementary years will contain the basics that will be elaborated later. By the time a young person has completed eight years of school he or she should know that: (1) stewardship affects everything in life; (2) a Christian uses resources carefully; (3) a Christian gives time and money to the church so others less fortunate or in need may be helped; and (4) a life based on Christian stewardship includes care for one's body as well as one's physical and social environment. The young person moving from an elementary to a youth class or department will have been taught to give money and time to the church, and to the church school, regularly.

2. Youth

Youth are typically considered by the church to be between fourteen and eighteen years of age. In some instances, persons who are nineteen are added to this group, especially if they happen to live near the church. Rarely will a twenty-year-old be included other than as a counselor for the youth group.

Youth are very conscious of their bodies, their possessions, and their proposed future. Stewardship education will deal with these topics in a general manner as it stresses the need to care for and preserve one's environment as well as one's body. This is quite important with regard to youth's desire to experiment with sex, alcohol, and drugs.

It is during these years that young people can be taken to work camps and be engaged in work projects. If they want to participate in a work camp, they should be required to raise their own money for transportation and to pay for their living needs at the camp. This program of self-support and working solely for others teaches them the value of money and friendship. It emphasizes that money can be hard to come by, especially by those who will benefit from the work camp.

Drama and firsthand stories as well as experience are methods of teaching that appeal to youth. They like to hear the dramatic presentation of the difference something has made to another person's life. Stewardship education can accommodate this need to be convinced by showing the results of giving as recounted by recipients of stewardship works. Many of these stories will be related to the tithe. It is impossible to program a disaster (and of course no one would want to), but stories of how youth helped by giving and sharing during disasters are also readily available. These stories are vivid and bring the message of stewardship home to them.

By the time a young person has reached age seventeen, he or she realizes a decision about a job, career, or continuing school must be made. It is unlikely that the decision will result in a lifelong vocation. In fact, a career choice may not be made until the young person's second full-time job. However, the church needs to include discussions about the stewardship of talents and time as part of the career selection process.

The school system will not deal with stewardship in career guidance courses because, from the school's point of view, the need is for a good job at a good wage. It is up to the church to make certain that young people understand sharing and giving as lifelong patterns for living and that these patterns should be incorporated into any career eventually selected.

The seriousness of boy-girl relationships at this time also makes it an arena in which stewardship should enter. The stewardship emphasis upon sharing, giving, and being responsible is very appropriate for these kinds of relationships. Young people are dealing with interpersonal concepts as they struggle to create life patterns. Their understanding of sharing, giving, and being responsible affects the kinds of commitments they believe are made between boys and girls or men and women. The ideas of stewardship should be forcefully presented in ways that show how they affect interpersonal relations until the concepts are understood.

Youth seldom like to deal with abstracts for extended periods of time. They are action oriented. They like truths about stewardship demonstrated through stories and people's lives. Because youth can translate theory into action, this age affords the church significant opportunities to discuss personal, social, and physical environmental issues that deal with stewardship. For example, recycling paper or aluminum may be economically profitable to a community, but youth can be taught the primary reason for recycling is not to generate money but to preserve one's environment. If they are encouraged to help set up a resource recovery and recycling process and are monitored as to their practices, preservation of natural resources becomes a practical as well as a theoretical issue for them.

3. Adults

Adulthood includes a wide array of ages and life circumstances in most churches. For example, young adults, at the lower end of the age spectrum, often are unmarried, are trying to complete an education or find a job or both, and are attempting to decide upon a lifetime career. For these persons, who are usually under twenty-five years of age, stewardship education is very much related to money and physical environment.

Persons between twenty-five and thirty-five years of age are the more settled young adults. They have begun a career, may be married and have a family, and may be growing roots in a community. They must be confronted with the stewardship implications of the use of their money, the use of their time, and the dedication of their lives to God. Budgeting should be a staple of the stewardship education program for them as might be courses or sessions on the creation of a personal financial plan.

As discussed in previous chapters, financial planning and wills are important parts of adult stewardship education. People must understand the need for them and the possible benefits these practices bring to themselves and to others. The stewardship education program for adults ought to include sessions on financial planning and will making.

TYPES OF EDUCATION NEEDED

Middle-aged adults, between thirty-five and fifty-five, have many obligations and opportunities to make money, spend money, and use their time. These people are in the age group from which the church and most other organizations like to draw their leaders. These adults must learn to choose between various opportunities for personal stewardship. Including "hard choices" in a stewardship education program can be very helpful to many adults in these years.

Older adults, those who have retired, need to know that their education and experiences ought to be shared at church with others. The accumulated experiences of older adults in a church can be a life's library for younger adults. Stewardship education for older persons must emphasize their need to share these experiences with others. This sharing is best done within the context of specific courses in which life experiences are relevant to the subject matter.

GENERAL PROGRAM NEEDS

A stewardship education program should not have a one-sided emphasis. Stewardship, as has been shown, encompasses money, time, and natural resources. A general program of stewardship education ought to incorporate these emphases through designing specific course offerings or materials for every age group.

It is likely that a general stewardship program has not been created in most congregations. They have relied on the every-member visitation or pledging program to educate people about stewardship. This does not work because these programs are too short and too focused on money. Even in those churches where time and talent cards are included in the pledging materials the primary focus of the campaign is on money.

Creating a stewardship education program will include items specific to each age group such as those discussed above. The design for the program will introduce stewardship concepts at early ages and then elaborate on them at later ages. Adults, in this educational design, will deal with a broad range of topics and experiences relating to money, time use, and natural resources. The method for handling the program at the adult level will probably be through short courses, workshops, or seminars. The point of the program, however, is to include money, time, and natural resources.

Handling and using money in an affluent society is a major concern to be addressed by the general stewardship education program. This is not meant to limit the discussions or emphases to money, but these issues must be raised. They cannot be raised during a pledge campaign because that is the wrong arena. The issues need to be broached and examined in a situation that is not tied to requests for giving. The issues are too important to be dismissed as a technique used by fund raisers to increase individual pledges.

Volunteering and its relationship to monetary gifts to and through the church is another topic needing to be addressed in a stewardship education program. The church depends upon people's gifts of time. The entire teaching program of most churches depends on the time and efforts of volunteers who are willing to be trained and to teach. The same can be said for the youth program, the women's program, the men's program, or any other substantive program in the church. In recognition of the continual need to recruit volunteers, the church should educate its membership in the careful use of time. This will enable members to better understand that giving time is an important part of good stewardship.

Programs for financial planning and wills, as have been discussed earlier, need to be included in a general stewardship program. An individual lives out his or her values by the way in which money is spent, time used, and resources handled. Church members ought to learn how a Christian steward does those things.

A general stewardship education program is not all that a church needs. Once this has been designed, it becomes essential to expand the vision of members to include concern for special areas of stewardship.

SPECIAL CONCERNS
OF STEWARDSHIP EDUCATION

Much has been said in recent years about being a good steward of one's environment. The argument is that the physical environment is finite, which means there is a beginning and an end to all resources. Because this is a fact, it is necessary to conserve those resources and replenish them when possible.

For instance, wood is finite. Forests have been depleted in certain parts of the world for use as firewood, building materials, or to sell. People have discovered that when forests are depleted land can erode and an economy can be seriously affected. Stewardship applied to forests has resulted in reforestation projects and scientific research to discover types of trees that grow quickly even in hostile terrain.

Energy is another exhaustible resource to which stewardship applies. Many congregations have sought to conserve energy by installing insulation in their buildings, turning off lights, setting the thermostat for higher temperatures in summer and lower in winter, and consolidating meetings. The impetus for such stewardship has been cost rather than theology in most cases. A good stewardship program however will enforce the money savings by examining energy use from a conserving point of view.

Land use is another type of stewardship issue that has not been given much attention by the church. Organizations outside the church have spent much time and energy teaching people how to farm with limited erosion. What has not been dwelt upon is the use of land for a variety of purposes. Zoning may be considered to be an attempt to limit land use, but zoning tends to enforce existing activities rather than promote good stewardship. A stewardship education program could raise issues about how land can and should be better used for the needs of people.

Including a special area of concern for stewardship may depend upon the location of a church. It is usually not appropriate for an inner city congregation to spend a great amount of time, for example, educating its members about the conservation of particular farm land. The needs and proximity of the congregation's environment tend to dictate other special concerns to be included in the stewardship education program. On the other hand, every church can expand its program of stewardship education by applying Jesus' message to its environment, whatever that environment happens to be.

SUMMARY

A stewardship education program must be age specific by dealing with issues in an understandable fashion for each age group. The program will also give attention to those areas of concern most likely to be felt by a given age group. A general stewardship program will include sessions on the Christian's use of money, time, and natural resources. The location and needs of a particular congregation will determine any additional stewardship concerns that must be included in the education program. However, energy conservation ought to be included in every church's stewardship education program. In an earlier chapter it was implied that a stewardship education program should not be limited to one time a year. The next chapter builds on that concept by outlining an emphasis on year-round stewardship.

Chapter 10

A YEAR-ROUND
STEWARDSHIP PROGRAM

The stewardship program of many congregations consists of a concentrated barrage of information at the time of the every-member visitation or when the budget is being underwritten. This intensive campaign focuses on money and emphasizes the need for people to give a percentage of their income to support the church. Some congregations may have a brief adult course during this period that deals with the tithe as the minimum of giving.

This is not a stewardship program as much as it is a promotional blitz. These churches use the word *stewardship* as a synonym for contributions of money to the church. This narrow definition of the word limits the perspective of church members and deprives them of opportunities to practice stewardship in other ways, such as giving time and conserving the environment. Although some of the literature used during the budget underwriting process might mention time, it is not a prime consideration in most fund-raising campaigns. Nor is stewardship of the environment, because very few references are made to this during stewardship campaigns of any type.

In addition to encompassing money, time, environments, and natural resources, a stewardship education program ought to be year-round. Its breadth, in fact, dictates that it be spread through an entire year. It might include a series of seminars for adults and a monthly session for children or youth. Other formats could include intensive week-long courses (held in the evenings) or weekend workshops for adults and youth as well as quarterly stewardship classes for children. This does not mean however that the program should be separated entirely from existing programs.

A stewardship education program is one component of a church's total Christian education program. Stewardship is not the sole topic for Christian education although it is a frequently neglected essential element. Pastors and church school leaders tend to ignore stewardship education because they believe it is a responsibility of the finance committee of the church. This relegation effectively eliminates any consideration of stewardship by Christian education persons, which in turn injures their program.

Stewardship education is designed to help people understand the practical implications of Jesus' teachings. Stewardship is an active, disciplined way of living. Stewardship education is a convergence of theory and practice. It requires biblical knowledge and the practice of spiritual disciplines. It focuses people's attention on the manner in which life's resources are to be used to the glory of God and the betterment of human kind. When understood from this perspective, a year-round stewardship education program becomes a way to focus energy for a Christian life pattern.

A stewardship education program should be integral to Christian education because it complements other elements of the broader educational curricula. It uses Bible study, describes interpersonal relationships in a new light, brings awareness of environmental and social issues, illuminates the need to conserve as well as to give, and emphasizes a life of discipline. Each of these is a part of

Christian education in general. Stewardship takes them out of stories and theories and puts them squarely into the daily lives of members.

The rationale for creating a stewardship education program on a year-round basis is one thing. Designing it is the key to making it effective. The design that follows seeks to relate this educational emphasis to existent programs in most churches. It is not to be considered an "add-on" in the sense that it is attached to existing programs. It should become integral to the church school, the budget building and underwriting process, and volunteer aspects of the church. Until this incorporation occurs, the stewardship education program will be an endangered and unattached program species in a church.

GETTING STARTED

A stewardship education program can begin any time; however, its logical initiation is when the church school starts its new year, usually in the fall. As with the church school curricula, stewardship education can be designed to coincide with the various church seasons, including Advent, Christmas, Epiphany, Lent, Easter, Pentecost, and Kingdomtide. During these seasons, stewardship education can help members focus on missions, church growth, and spiritual development.

A stewardship education program may be built around the concepts of steward, tithe, first fruits, and jubilee (as described in *The Tithe: Challenge or Legalism?*). These concepts can be used each season with slightly different emphases. The general design for such a program, as outlined below, can be adapted to the style of a specific congregation.

Fall is a preparation time for the budget underwriting process in most congregations. This may be a pledge campaign or a series of letters asking members and friends to give regularly to the church as they prepare their own budgets for the coming year. This period in a stewardship education program will focus primarily on money and can include a series of pamphlets and booklets about proportionate giving and tithing. These materials may be mailed or otherwise distributed to the members. In some situations, the materials will be used in classes or workshops on financial planning or both. The literature should cover the essentials of how to compute giving on the basis of various percentages, including the tithe. Also the literature should suggest volunteer work as a means of expressing commitment through the church.

This is a good time to offer one or two sessions on personal financial planning in adult and youth church school classes. Financial planning helps people think about money and provides them with techniques to create strategies for its use, including giving. These sessions may be held during the regular church school time or offered as optional or additional sessions. Usually it is best to have a leader whose background has equipped him or her to work with people in the specifics of budgeting, tax planning, and a financially conserving life pattern.

In addition to financial planning workshops and sending literature through the mail, two or three sermons might be built around the theme of stewardship. These sermons should help people understand the broader concepts of stewardship specifically related to giving time, using resources, and conserving the environment. However, if the sermons are designed to be a part of the every-member visitation program the temptation of the pastor will be to deal with money only. This is acceptable only when additional courses or literature underlining the importance of other forms of stewardship are made available.

Thanksgiving, Advent, and Christmas are ideal times to teach about the use of resources to better the life situations of others. Special collections of money, food, and clothing during these seasons are techniques familiar to most church members. Money and commodities are visible signs of sharing but often are not accompanied by information about the needs of those receiving assistance, the continuing outreach efforts of the congregation, or the programs of the organizations that are given the money and commodities. A stewardship education program should stress the need to give, as well as provide information about the organizations receiving the gifts and the outreach programs of the church, so that giving does not end immediately after Christmas.

For example, Thanksgiving-Advent-Christmas is a season when sharing information about the activities of retirement homes, hospitals, urban ministries, and special projects of the congregation can become a major part of the stewardship education program. People will want to give, and information acquired through stewardship education classes can help them know the extent and type of ministries they are involved in through their congregation and denomination.

Epiphany and Lent are seasons during which stewardship can be related specifically to life patterns and spiritual disciplines. The stewardship education emphasis during this extended church season should not be on money as much as it is on developing a giving life pattern. The giving life pattern focuses on use of time and may suggest involvement in outreach work projects, active participation in community outreach programs of the congregation, and volunteer activity in the local church by serving on committees or teaching in the church or visiting within the parish. The application of stewardship principles to the use of time blends well with the Lenten emphasis on self-discipline.

Easter and Pentecost are times in a stewardship education program to discuss missions and social environments. The emphasis at this time is on expanding the ministry of the church. The stewardship education message is how one supports and becomes involved in this expansion. Classes can emphasize the use of time through volunteering but can also work on interpersonal relations. The stories of Easter and Pentecost are personal testimonies of the effect that individuals and small groups can have on their world. The use of one's life to exemplify the teachings of Jesus Christ is the stewardship issue to be discussed during this period.

Church growth occurs as people witness to others and convince them that the church has a message that can change their lives. The stewardship concept of commitment in relationship to personal witnessing can be discussed at this time. This period of stewardship education can focus almost entirely on tithing in its various forms.

Kingdomtide, the months between Pentecost and Advent, is a time to focus on stewardship of the environment. This is the summer season, when many people are more aware of their physical surroundings than at other periods of the year. Education about the need to conserve and preserve is useful in assisting people to better understand the need to have a life pattern of stewardship toward their physical surroundings.

Starting a year-round stewardship education program means creating a calendar in which specific stewardship emphases are inserted. This process of planning is simplified when the church year is followed. This allows stewardship emphases to become integral to all church and Christian education programs rather than being grafted onto a few parts of one or the other program.

COMPLEMENTING THE EVERY-MEMBER VISITATION

A year-round stewardship education program will benefit the church significantly in two ways at every-member visitation time. The first benefit will be in recruiting persons to work on the every-member visit. During the year the subject of volunteering will have been approached from the viewpoints of steward, tithing, first fruits, and jubilee. The discussions and presentations around these themes with regard to using time will make recruiting easier for church work, including participation in the every-member visitation program. Second, these viewpoints will also have been involved in discussions about use of money, which ought to be reflected in the amounts of money people give to the church.

These general benefits from a year-round program can be bolstered by (1) financial planning, which includes budgeting for giving; (2) computing proportionate giving to the church; and (3) a serious consideration of tithing. These three specifics can be considered in depth during the every-member visitation period. They must be designed for differing groups within the congregation. For example, it is certain that not everyone will need or be interested in a course on financial planning. Thus, a course should be designed specifically for those who feel they want and need it. The situation will differ also for courses or workshops offered on tithing. The group attending these sessions might be quite limited in number. On the other hand, everyone will need to know about proportionate giving, especially during the every-member visitation program. This topic will be handled differently than financial planning and tithing.

Financial planning courses during an every-member visitation preparation period can be quite helpful to those in the congregation who have never budgeted or lived by the discipline of a budget. The attendees will be instructed in the techniques of budget building, methods for creating realistic spending habits, developing a means for saving, and learning how to give. The previous chapters on financial planning can assist in the design of these courses or workshops.

A congregation with every member being a tither is a hope of many churches. This is unfortunate because most persons can give more than 10 percent of their income and still live quite well. Even so, emphasizing the tithe as a standard of giving during an every-member visitation program can be very helpful to church members. The class will focus on the tithe as a benchmark for giving. This emphasis will be a welcome addition to the stewardship education program of most churches.

Materials outlining proportionate giving, especially pamphlets, are used in most churches to guide people in deciding how much of their income to give to the church. These materials usually include a chart detailing how much a gift would amount to if an individual decided on one of several different percentages of weekly or monthly take-home income. Rarely do these charts include money earned on investments or royalties that are paid annually or quarterly. The assumption underlying these materials is that individuals can compute percentages of quarterly or annual income on their own by using the chart. A more realistic procedure would be to include in the materials a method for computing percentages of giving regardless of when income is received.

These materials, in addition to being limited to computations of weekly or monthly income, must usually be revised to offset the assumption that all income is earned. Many people receive benefits from a governmental agency, pension funds, or an annuity. These benefits ought to be included with any other income they receive when people compute their giving to the church. Assisting everyone to understand how to compute a percentage of their income or their benefits to give to the church can be a goal of a class, workshop, or pamphlets distributed the every-member visitation program This will expand most people's concepts of giving.

The every-member visitation program, then, can be enhanced considerably by year-round stewardship education. The two benefits, better recruitment and more giving, may be realized without additional classes or courses. However, every-member visitation time can make classes and courses on financial planning, tithing, and proportionate giving more effective. The direct results of these classes can be measured by the giving patterns of members during the campaign.

WORKING WITH THE CHURCH SCHOOL

Church school curricula do not generally contain stewardship themes because stewardship education has been considered to be a responsibility of the finance committee in most churches and denominations. Thus, denominational educational materials on stewardship must be ordered separately and from a different place than are Christian education curriculum materials. In most denominations, the Stewardship Office of one of the boards must be asked for these materials.

The pastor will have to work with congregational educational leaders in order to integrate stewardship emphases into the church's educational program. A decision to work out such integration should be made jointly by the education and the finance or stewardship committees. These separate committee actions will then be confirmed by the church board. Such formalities, while bothersome and time consuming, are important because without them one committee or the other might feel threatened and become defensive about someone else doing its job.

After these legislative procedures are perfomed, a joint committee can be formed to design a year-round stewardship education program with specific classes or courses. Several of the classes and courses may become part of the regular church school offerings; others may be "specials" sponsored by the joint committee. This procedure of integration and special classes allows both the education committee and the finance or stewardship committee to claim sponsorship and to be responsible for stewardship education.

Church school teachers for all age groups will need to be trained in stewardship concepts. Training sessions separate from those normally conducted for teachers can be used to acquaint church school personnel with stewardship education emphases and the concepts of steward, first fruits, tithe, and jubilee. The teachers should also be encouraged to attend the special classes and workshops open to members and friends of the congregation.

The committee responsible for stewardship education should review and make available leaflets, booklets, films, videotapes, and audiotapes for each age group and special interest group in the church. These materials will add to the educational literature given to children, youth, and adults in the normal course of the church school experience. Stewardship literature can be added to the racks that contain free take-home materials, at the rear of the sanctuary or by the church office.

It is critical for proponents of stewardship education to work closely with the church school because this is a regular avenue for the church to get into many homes. Furthermore, people expect the church school to teach them and to give them materials to take home for study. These are the elements necessary for a stewardship education program to succeed.

POSTERS, DISPLAYS, LITERATURE, SERMONS

People need signs to help them remember. Posters and displays are used often in the church as reminders and should become ways in which people are taught about stewardship. Posters and displays can be used much like a teacher uses bulletin boards to teach and remind pupils of assignments and current topics of study. The effectiveness of the posters and displays depends on how frequently they are changed as well as their attractiveness. A current and attractive poster or display can be a valuable addition to a stewardship education program.

Posters can be placed almost anywhere in the church building. Usually they are taped (with masking tape) to the rear wall of a sanctuary or any other wall, placed in the fellowship hall, and put in strategic locations in the church school. Several of the posters can be identical, but a series of posters with differing themes may be more desirable. Except for those for the every-member visitation program, such posters should be designed and made by the church. This personalized effort helps the church focus on its emphases.

Displays tend to be for bulletin boards, tables near literature racks, or both. A display includes several types of items, such as pamphlets, posters, photographs, booklets, and books. These can be arranged around a theme. For example, a committee designing a year-round stewardship education program will use the theme of the season as the basis for its displays.

A display table is an ideal vehicle for distributing free literature. People who look at and can take a pamphlet with them are more likely to be informed than those who look at but cannot take any literature with them. An admonishment to a committee working with displays is to keep take-home materials available on the display tables.

Liberal quantities of literature should be ordered by a church for its stewardship education program. This literature can be used as inserts in the weekly or monthly newsletter that is mailed to members' homes, as inserts in the Sunday morning worship bulletin, and as pieces people can take with them as they leave the church building. A committee will want to follow a schedule that rotates literature so that its appeal is not lost by remaining the same for several weeks or months. The committee might want to use inserts once a month or quarter as a means of emphasizing or concluding a class or churchwide study course.

Making literature available to members will cost money. A pamphlet can be purchased for a minimal price when it is ordered in quantity. A church should not be frightened by a price tag, because every type of education is expensive. The church ought to look at the long-range possibilities rather than short-term obligations when it decides on how many different kinds and the quantities of free stewardship literature to provide its members.

Sermons are usually the responsibility of pastors. It is appropriate, however, for laypersons to create and deliver sermons. This is especially true for stewardship topics. For instance, it is more powerful for a layperson to speak about tithing than it is for a pastor. People expect this type of message from the pastor, but it is more realistic coming from a layperson who practices tithing. Quarterly sermons on a stewardship topic, whether delivered by the pastor or a layperson, should be part of a year-round stewardship education program.

SUMMARY

A year-round stewardship education program is not a luxury as much as it is a necessity for a church that is serious about the life pattern of its members. The best method for planning a stewardship education program is to relate it to the church year. This affords it the same general emphasis that other church programming has. It can begin at any time of the year but may be more consistent with other programs if it begins in the fall. The stewardship education emphasis should be designed with the same care and foresight that goes into the Christian education program. In fact, it should be integrated into the Christian education program as well as offer special sessions on particular topics such as wills. A good stewardship education program will complement the every-member visitation emphasis by providing courses in budgeting, proportionate giving, and tithing at the appropriate times. Church school teachers will need training in stewardship themes and instruction in how to include those themes in their normal curricula. Visual aids such as posters and displays should include free literature so that people may take it home for later reading and study. At least quarterly, sermons ought to be preached on stewardship themes. Visual aids, literature, and sermons should be carefully designed to support the total stewardship education program of the congregation.

Chapter 11

PROGRAM BUDGETING

Budgets are uncommon in many churches. Pastors and laypersons often do not think they need budgets. In these congregations the leaders decide what the church wants to do and then they do it. People, including some who tithe, give what they feel they should, and when more money is needed the pastor mentions the need from the pulpit. People respond to the request and the program goes on as intended.

This kind of church operation may seem chaotic to other pastors. They feel a church should have goals, program planning, and accurate budgeting procedures. These pastors include in the budget everything related to any program. They even make allowances for unforeseen events by adding an item called "contingencies." They see themselves as prudent and farsighted in the use of church resources. These same pastors tend to be regarded, by members and pastors in churches that are much less formal in budgeting, as insecure and of little faith.

These two groups of pastors are at opposite poles with regard to planning and budgeting in the church. Most churches and pastors live between these two extremes. There is no question that goals, planning, budgeting, and using effective fund-raising techniques to underwrite a budget in the church are important. Churches that function without goals and budgets are amiss in their stewardship education procedures. Goals encourage church members to strive for particular achievements. Budgets, by explaining their current status, can be used to inform members about program costs. In addition, a budget, because it separates income and expenditures into specific line items, allows church leaders to plan for program innovation or helps them decide where to cut back in case of a drop-off in giving.

The fact that everything the church does has a cost is subconsciously accepted by church people. This fact is brought into their consciousness through the process of budget building. A budget helps members feel that they make a difference in the church's life when they make a contribution because they can see the needs by reading the budget. A budget can be used to keep members informed of the exact costs and status of each program. A set of goals, a plan, and a budget are vehicles for helping members understand what their church is trying to do and assisting them in contributing meaningfully to their church.

A church budget normally deals with the actual cash income and expenditures for each given service or activity. For instance, the church school budget might include costs for having someone conduct a training program for teachers, the purchase of curriculum and related items, and rental costs for visual or audio aids. These expenses would generally be lumped together under the line item "church school" in a church budget. In the same manner, expenses for the office—duplication, telephone, and so forth—would be listed as separate entries.

A more complex form of budgeting is program budgeting. Program budgeting extends the concept of budgets to include every item that may be needed to put a program into effect. In program budgeting, contributions and expenditures are not restricted to money but include estimated volunteer time, money and time for any form of outreach by church members, estimates of the time for teachers and administrators who work in the church school, and so forth. A program budget would add the value of time contributed by volunteer teachers and administrators in the church school to the line item "church school." Within the education committee budget, which is part of the church school line item in the church budget, another set of line items would identify expenses for administration of the church school; curriculum and teaching costs for the children, youth, and adult segments of the church school program; teacher training, equipment, and supplies; and any other items needed to make the school effective.

A program budget also identifies all needs and expenses incurred by every program. For instance, a pastor's time (and its cost) is divided into various line items in a budget and added to each one as an expense. If a pastor is paid $20,000 (including housing) a year and spends one-fourth of his or her time working with the church school, the program budget would allocate one-fourth, or $5,000, of the pastor's support to the church school line item.

The aim of program budgeting is to present an accurate picture of all needs and expenses of every type of program sponsored by a church. It is a laudable goal, but one by the way that is quite difficult to achieve. The program budget concept was initiated and used for a time by the Department of Defense as a way to maintain control of its budget. It proved however to be a cumbersome and unrealistic method for planning and budgeting. It took too much time and energy to create the budget and monitor the expenses. Budget builders had to guess so often about percentages and values of time that the budget was not reliable. It was deemed unworkable and was scrapped.

In spite of the government's decision to eliminate it as a planning model, program budgeting has been tried by various church bodies. They have felt that it was a good business planning model and could be useful, with some modifications, in the church. A few advocates remain enthusiastic about it, but it has generally not been effective for churches or church agencies. It is often too cumbersome and unreliable to be useful.

Attempting to create a program budget nevertheless can be helpful in demonstrating the breadth of a church's program. For example, a modified form of a program budget can assist a church in estimating the cost of specific projects. A church may use program budgeting to estimate its investment in an outreach program such as a food pantry. Cash expenses are limited inasmuch as food stuffs are donated, space for storage and disbursement of commodities is found in the church building, and volunteers are recruited to manage the pantry. A program budget would estimate the value of time, space, and commodities in order to determine the income and the cost to the church for the program. The theory behind the estimates and budget for this project is that people who give to the food pantry and who manage it could possibly give time and money to other church sponsored programs.

In fact, however, a church functions quite differently from what is anticipated by a program budget. A church does not attach cash values to donated time, nor is it interested in doing so. It is likely that people who volunteer to manage a food pantry quite often would not work in similar capacities in other church related programs. The meaning of working in the church goes far beyond the estimates of costs.

Program budgeting is designed to work within the framework of overarching organizational goals. A program budget assumes that the organization is confronted with many pressing needs and has limited funds with which to meet those needs. Therefore the overarching goals, as supported in the program budget, represent the organization's only program endeavors. As one can see, the theory underlying a program budget makes it attractive to the church. However, the church has means other than overarching goals to work out the allocation of monies and energies. A program budget, because it is based on a mentality of limits, does not fit well with the church that feels it must challenge its members to give more time and money to meet the multiple needs of its people and community.

This is not to suggest that goals are not important and that money and energy ought not to be allocated. The simple fact is that the process by which these are established and accomplished within most churches is not through program budgeting. Even so, there are aspects of program budgeting that can be used by most congregations. These include its use in stewardship education and its emphasis upon goal and evaluation.

USING PROGRAM BUDGETING IN STEWARDSHIP EDUCATION

Stewardship education is concerned with the use of time, money, and natural resources. A program budget is also interested in these articles when they relate to specific church activities. The illustration of the food pantry project indicates one way a program budget calculates people's use of time as a contribution as well as an expense in a church budget. Because they include time and money as both income and expense, program budgets can be used as educational aids for stewardship classes.

One way to use program budgets in stewardship education is to have people in a financial planning class design a personal program budget. Converting their use of time into cost equivalents can be very instructive. The class may require each person to keep track of his or her time use for a week or two. This is done by making notations in a notebook at fifteen-minute intervals per day for seven to fourteen days. At the end of the week or weeks, the individual is asked to calculate the dollar equivalents of time spent in church work, in doing nothing, in exercising, and so forth. These kinds of data show the individual's current life pattern and may assist in making changes in how energies are used, which is the point of the class.

Another use of a program budget for a church can be in stewardship education classes on tithing and proportionate giving. The church's program budget shows the proposed program of the church in terms of time needs as well as money requirements. In addition to pointing out that volunteering time is crucial to the church's program, a program budget identifies the amount of time needed to carry out specific programs. This delineation of time needs can influence how much money and energy people are willing to give. Using the program budget in this fashion, as an illustrative tool in stewardship education classes during the budget underwriting period, can provide a guide for church members to follow while they consider how much of their time and money to give to the church.

A third use of a program budget in stewardship education is to create a series of three different program budgets for a class in tithing. A low budget would represent the church's program as it currently exists, including time and money contributions. A medium budget would be somewhat higher and demonstrate the effect of 5 percent of the church members as tithers of their time and money. A high budget would be further increased to show the probable effect on the church's program if 10 percent of the members became tithers of their time and money. These projected program budgets could produce great excitement within the congregation because they would illustrate the effects of personal commitment of time as well as of money to the church.

A program budget, as these illustrations suggest, can be a teaching tool in the stewardship education program. Program budgets are to be created with real projections but are not generally implemented as such. The reason for this is that it is usually impractical for churches to live by a program budget.

LIMITATIONS OF PROGRAM BUDGETING AS A PRACTICAL BUDGETING DEVICE

A program budget is not practical because it takes too much time and energy to design and implement in most congregations. In those where it may be practical, the churches are not interested. In addition, the program budget has been ineffective in churches that have attempted to use it.

A small congregation does not have enough of a program to make program budgeting useful. In many of these churches, the pastor's salary consumes between one-third and two-thirds of the cash budget. In effect, the pastor becomes the program since it is up to him or her to recruit, train, and activate volunteers as workers in the church. Dividing up costs of the pastor into various budgetary line items does little to enhance the program or offset the fact that supporting a pastor is the largest part of a budget. In these churches, program budgeting is considered to be a waste of time.

Creating a program budget in a medium-sized congregation (300 to 1,000 members) takes a great deal of time and much guesswork. A possible value in trying to do a program budget is the discipline of creating churchwide goals toward which each organization's goals can contribute. A second value may be to assist a congregation to decide to realign its program so that it ministers more effectively to its community. The primary drawback is that medium-sized churches tend to be limited in program possibilities both by their environment and by the available resources (time and money) of the members. Goal setting and normal budgeting are a more realistic approach for these churches.

Large congregations have staff enough to work on a program budget because it takes time and energy from full-time employees to make it useful as a planning and monitoring device. But in these churches, staff members are assigned specialties and few have enough energy to assume the task of working on a program budget. In addition, estimating the value and use of time by the many volunteers is quite complex. Evaluation and monitoring are needs that tend to be met through existing committees and the church board does the planning for the church.

These major limitations to program budgeting, as the above illustrations suggest, are the time and the energy needed to create and maintain it. A staff person who can devote much time to helping create it and to keeping track of its various aspects once it is adopted is essential if it is to be effective. Most churches are unwilling or unable to assign a staff member to this task. What is more, congregations can do their evaluations and goal setting in a less stringent fashion and still accomplish what they desire.

The theme of evaluation has run through this discussion of program budgeting. This emphasis on evaluation might be the most significant contribution this type of planning can make to the church.

UTILIZING PROGRAM BUDGETING'S EMPHASIS ON EVALUATION

One of the serious problems with church programming is its lack of consistent and regular evaluation. Most churches, in fact, do very little evaluation. Programs continue for years with few attempts to determine if they are fulfilling the goals or objectives of the church. It usually takes a crisis of some sort for serious evaluation to be used in a church.

A congregation, in order to use evaluation effectively, needs to set goals and plan its program. This is the way it sets a direction for its program. Once it has goals and a plan, the church can evaluate its program to decide whether it is doing what it feels is most important in its community, with its members, and in the world. Even if there is no formal goal-setting process on which to base evaluation, someone within the church knows the directions and emphases the congregation wants to pursue. These informal goals are as significant as formal goals.

Evaluation is possible only when there are goals or at least some anticipations toward which a program is aimed. For example, an evangelism program may establish a goal of winning ten new people to Christ and the church during a three-month period. A cursory evaluation of this program is rather easy: One can count the number of those won to Christ and the church during this period. Evaluation of discrete programs such as underwriting the budget or raising the attendance average in church school and church is also relatively simple. Numbers are the goals. When the program time period is over, a review of the numbers constitutes the evaluation. The church either underwrites its budget or it does not, and it increases its average attendance or it does not.

Suppose it doesn't meet one of these goals. Shouldn't the church look for possible reasons for the failure? Most of the time a few leaders will give some excuses for why the goals were not reached, but seldom is there an evaluation of the total program so that actual reasons for failure can be pinpointed. This lack of evaluation makes it improbable that changes in the program will be made.

Evaluation is threatening to many people. This is unfortunate. An evaluation process ought to assist people to make changes in the church's approach and programming. An evaluation is not a witch hunt nor is it to discredit an individual. Seldom is one person the cause of a program's failure. The atmosphere of a church, which is composed of the attitudes of every member, is usually a main culprit. Saying that the attitudes of members ought to be changed does not blame anyone in particular but suggests that everyone can be responsible for changing the church.

Evaluation can be stringent but does not need to be. It

must be consistent and done for all programs. Evaluation of music programs should not exclude one choir. Nor should it focus on the professionalism of the choir members. Such an evaluation might deal with the types of music provided or needing to be provided, the expense of the program in relationship to other programs of the church, and the kind of professionalism required of the leader. Even a sensitive program such as music can be evaluated without it becoming personal.

It is important to understand that programs need changing and some ought to be discontinued. A church must constantly change if it is to minister effectively to its membership and its community. The program budget was designed to help organizations make those changes through goal setting and evaluating. Even though program budgets may not be feasible, evaluation should be used in every church regularly. Evaluating the needs of members and the community helps a church create goals and formulate more effective programs.

Even though a program budget may be impractical for most churches, its emphasis on evaluation should be embraced as an important additive. Indeed, evaluation is a critical exercise for every living congregation.

SUMMARY

A program budget seeks to identify all needs and expenses of every program, including time and money. In this regard, it can be a useful tool for individuals and churches when they assess their life patterns. Program budgeting, however, because it is time-consuming and unreliable, is impractical for most uses in churches. The emphasis of program budgeting on setting goals, planning, and evaluating is crucial to the church. While the form in which this emphasis is carried out may be different from program budgeting, the need should not be lost on any congregation.

Resources

The following lists of offices and materials are suggestive and not definitive. Resources are produced regularly for each of the kinds of stewardship and finance discussed in this book.

DENOMINATIONAL STEWARDSHIP OFFICES

American Baptist Churches in the USA, Valley Forge, PA 19481.
Christian Church (Disciples of Christ), 222 S. Downey Ave., Box 1986, Indianapolis, IN 46206.
Church of the Brethren, 1451 Dundee Ave., Elgin, IL 60120.
The Episcopal Church, 815 Second Ave., New York, NY 10117.
Presbyterian Church (USA), 475 Riverside Dr., 12th floor, New York, NY 10115.
United Church of Christ, 105 Madison Ave., New York, NY 10116.
The United Methodist Church, Board of Discipleship, P. O. Box 840 (1908 Grand Ave.), Nashville, TN 37202.

FUND RAISING

Office of Finance and Field Service, General Board of Global Ministries, 475 Riverside Dr., 3rd floor, New York, NY 10115.

SELECTED BOOKS

Carlson, Martin E. *Why People Give*. New York: Friendship Press, 1968.

Gustafson, James M. *Treasure in Earthen Vessels—The Church as a Human Community.* New York: Harper and Brothers, 1961.

Holck, Manfred, Jr. *Clergy Desk Book.* Nashville: Abingdon Press, 1985.

Hall, Douglas John. *The Steward: A Biblical Symbol Come of Age.* New York: Friendship Press, 1982.

Johnson, Douglas W. *The Care and Feeding of Volunteers.* Nashville: Abingdon, 1978.

————. *Let's Be Realistic About Your Church Budget.* Valley Forge, Pa.: Judson Press, 1984.

————. *The Tithe: Challenge or Legalism?* Nashville: Abingdon Press, 1984.

————. *A Workbook for Futuring and Goalsetting.* General Board of Global Ministries, The United Methodist Church, 1986.

Schaller, Lyle E. *Hey, That's Our Church!* Nashville: Abingdon, 1975.

Walker, Joe W. *Money in the Church.* Nashville: Abingdon, 1982.

A Stewardship Bibliography published by the Commission on Stewardship, National Council of the Churches of Christ in the U.S.A. (1985). 475 Riverside Dr., 8th floor, New York, NY 10115.